The
Lindsay Whalen
Story

"I never had the chance to get to know Lindsay until she reported to training camp this spring. The first thing that jumped out at me, and continues to impress me, is how much she has stayed herself. In this case what everyone has to say about an athlete is true—Lindsay has an amazing gift to just be real. And that gift lets her communicate comfortably with anybody from toddlers to senior citizens. She has a gift for making people feel special. Lindsay is a special player and a special person and I am glad she has the chance to be back in Minnesota to enrich all of our lives."

Roger Griffith,
Executive V.P.& CFO/Chief Operating Officer, Minnesota Lynx

"Lindsay Whalen is the epitome of a professional athlete—hard working, a student of the game, and a role model to girls and boys alike. She takes nothing for granted and her gift as an athlete pales in comparrison to her good nature, sense of humor and sense of being. She is a true all star on and off the court."

Chris Sienko,
Vice President, General Manager, WNBA Connecticut Sun

"I consider it my good fortune to have worked with Lindsay Whalen for six seasons, from 2004 to 2009, as she evolved from a promising rookie into a WNBA All Star. Even in the early days of her first season, you could see she was going to be special. But it didn't take long to realize that for all of her greatness on the court, Lindsay the player was always going to be a distant second to Lindsay the person. I can't think of any higher praise."

Bill Tavares,
Media Relations Manager, WNBA Connecticut Sun

"When you have players that change your life in a profound way they are special. The hardest thing to be now days is REAL. Lindsay has never lived her life worrying about what someone might think, she lives her life worrying about doing the right thing. When you live your life worrying about and doing the right thing, you end up being that special person that changes lives in a wonderful way. Thanks Lindsay."

Andy Rostberg,
Coach, Hutchinson High School

"The Gopher women's basketball program was almost invisible until this quiet, shy young woman from Hutchinson showed up on campus and made it the hottest ticket in the Twin Cities. I think it's safe to say the Lindsay Whalen did more for her sport than any athlete at the University of Minnesota in the 25 years I covered sports in this town."

Joe Schmit,
Anchor and Sports Director of KSTP's 5 Eyewitness News

"When you mention the great basketball names in Minnesota, Whalen deserves to be mentioned with George Mikan, Kevin McHale, Mychal Thompson and Kevin Garnett. She put Minnesota Gopher basketball on the NCAA map in 2004, when she carried the U of M to the Final Four. Whalen is a role model for young athletes all across Minnesota. Her success on and off the basketball floor is impressive."

Eric Nelson,
Sports Host and Reporter, WCCO Minneapolis

"Whalen is a great role model and a perfect example that with hard work and dedication, dreams can and do come true. She is a very caring person (with a great sense of humor) that never forgot her roots."

John Mons,
Operations Manager, KDUZ/KARP Radio, Hutchinson

"I look forward, in 25 or so years, to sitting with grandchildren and telling them I knew Lindsay Whalen, like the way my parents and grandparents talked about seeing Harmon Killebrew hit a home run into the next row, or how they were in attendance at Bert Blyleven's major league debut. I remember hearing this line somewhere that I feel is fitting for her … 'Legends get remembered, but heroes never die'… Lindsay is a hero to all of us."

Joel Niemeyer,
Sports Director/Assistant Program Coordinator, KDUZ/KARP Radio

"Lindsay changed women's basketball and it's perception at the University of Minnesota, not just because of her play, but the way she handled herself to the public."

Mike Max,
Anchor of WCCO Sports Tonight with Mike Max

"Lindsey Whalen is the best Women's College Basketball player I've covered in 30 years of reporting in Minnesota. She brings intensity without ego."

Larry Fitzgerald
National Programming Network- Almanac-TPT

The
Lindsay Whalen
Story

R. S. Oatman

NODIN PRESS

Photo credits:
All photos are from the Whalen family collection except as follows:
Hutchinson *Leader,* 18, 50, 52 (photo by Eric Kraushar)
University of Minnesota, 30, 34, 39, 135
Kim Danlo, 15, 37, 58, 88 (top)
Cathy Mahowald, 41, 45, 48, 164
Sophia Hantzes, 128

Design: John Toren
Cover photo: Sophia Hantzes

ISBN: 978-1-935666-16-5
Library of Congress Control Number: 2010935969

Nodin Press, LLC
530 North Third Street
Suite 120
Minneapolis, MN
55401

To Ben and our families,
to friends and fans,
with all my love and gratitude

– Lindsay

CONTENTS

FOREWORD

It's safe to say that no other student-athlete has ever had the impact on Golden Gopher athletic history that Lindsay Whalen did in her basketball career at the University of Minnesota. As the years pass since a shy Hutchinson kid became a household name throughout the state of Minnesota, those of us lucky enough to be along for the ride have come to appreciate more and more just what Lindsay did for the university, the state, and thousands of young, aspiring athletes.

Lindsay will always be remembered as the standout on a team that brought magic and huge crowds to Williams Arena, #13 jerseys too numerous to count, and of course the unforgettable trip to the Final Four in 2004. She and her teammates turned Gopher women's basketball games into the hottest ticket in town. The media loved her unassuming demeanor and jumped on the bandwagon following a Cinderella story that first began in her sophomore season and concluded on the highest stage of collegiate basketball.

A great thing about Lindsay is that she not only put in the hard work necessary to be successful, she possesses that rare ability to make those around her so much better. It's easy to forget that Lindsay helped forge the tradition of Gopher basketball playing under three head coaches, or that she wasn't a highly recruited superstar out of high school. Or, that if she weren't smaller in stature in her youth, ice hockey would likely have been her sport of choice.

Thankfully, basketball won out, and now one only has to look to the rafters of The Barn where a banner of Lindsay, floating through the air for a fingertip layup, is a constant reminder of the legacy #13 left behind. Stand at center court of the famed raised floor of Williams Arena and close your eyes. You can see the effortless no-look passes or the fear-defying drives to the basket, and hear the deafening pulse of an excited Gopher following.

The shining moment I'll remember forever wasn't the fantastic journey to New Orleans for the Final Four or the awe-inspiring upset of No. 1 Duke in the regional final. Instead it was the triumphant return of Lindsay, after a broken hand midway through her senior season that threatened to leave this story without the fairy tale ending.

Minnesota earned its third consecutive trip to the NCAA Championships and was selected to host the first and second rounds. The only talk that week was, would Lindsay play, could Lindsay play? Unable to withstand the unknown, Gopher fans packed into The Barn and welcomed their beloved team onto the floor. Not for the tipoff, but for the earliest of team warm-ups. One would have thought the game had already started, but no, Lindsay had just made a simple layup. She was going to play. By the time the team returned to the floor, Minnesota flags flying, for their final pregame routine, the crowd had worked its way into a frenzy. Williams Arena was pounding with electricity.

UCLA ran into a buzz-saw that night. One of the most famous gestures in Gopher basketball lore occurred early in that game. Lindsay netted a three-point field goal and running back on defense raised her broken right hand as if to say, "Yeah, I'm just fine." The crowd erupted once again. Truth be known, that was just a defensive call. Lindsay scored 31 points in the game and that magical run to the Final Four was on!

The memories Lindsay provided Minnesota basketball fans may not be her greatest legacy. What blossomed from her career was a generation of young basketball players, both girls and boys, who wanted to play just like Lindsay.

To this day, she continues to be a shining star of a role model; no greater tribute for a Gopher alum. Lindsay may have scored more points than any other player in Minnesota history, but more so, she owns a special place in the hearts of so many Gopher fans.

Lindsay Whalen will forever be a Golden Gopher. She always gave her all, but we were truly the lucky ones. She took us along on an amazing ride.

To Lindsay, all we can say is thank you.

– Joel Maturi,
Athletic Director, University of Minnesota

Young Lindsay on her way to the hockey rink.

1

EARLY SIGNS OF A STAR

Lindsay Marie Whalen, one of the most popular and influential players in women's basketball history, was born in Hutchinson, Minnesota, an hour west of Minneapolis, on May 9, 1982, to Neil and Kathryn Whalen. The first-born of the five Whalen children, Lindsay spent her early years in Hutchinson, a town of thirteen thousand where neighbors know neighbors, the new mixes with old, and the clock on Main Street keeps the pace flowing.

Hutchinson, like others of its kind, is a bustling Midwestern town with traditions, values, and people with goals and aspirations to be their best. From Hutchinson have come four NFL players: Lydon Murtha of the Miami Dolphins; Mitch Erickson, Seattle Seahawks; Nate Swift, Jacksonville Jaguars, and Cory Sauter, former quarterback and current coach at Southwest Minnesota State. From the town also are Roman Catholic Bishop John Jeremiah McRaith, recently retired, and four star Army General, former head of the United States Army Training and Doctrine Command, John W. Foss.

And, of course, Lindsay Whalen.

Lindsay's heart is grounded in sports, Hutchinson, Minnesota, and family, which makes the trade to her home state WNBA Lynx, an arrangement six years in the doing, a sweet deal indeed. Happy as she is that it has happened, she holds no regrets or misgivings about the twists and turns her career took in that interval.

"There's a reason and right timing for everything," she says.

That attitude and philosophy is a large part of her appeal and success, and explains why her game play, so full of surprise at every turn, so precisely maneuvered and dead-on in aim, has always captivated the crowds who flock to watch her. The combination of her magical plays and the power behind her reserved, humble demeanor together create Lindsay's greatness.

She has had that demeanor since early childhood, along with her desire for all things sports related. At an age when most children focus primarily on toys, Lindsay was already a "wannabe" athlete. For reasons she didn't yet know, she'd get excited each time her parents' car passed the Metrodome. Her excitement was audible, and before long the family joined in with a car game to see who could spot the Dome first. Then came her first Viking game in the Dome to seal the deal for little Lindsay. She was hooked.

"My Aunt Mary took me to one game every season and it was always a highlight of the year for me. I would go into the cities on Saturday and stay at her house. She always took me somewhere for dinner, usually at Champs. And then we would hit the Dome for the game on Sunday. I always got a thrill seeing the field and watching the teams warm up. I loved going to those games! I always wanted to go on the field for some reason. I just thought that would be the coolest thing to get to walk on the Metrodome field."

She would someday get that chance. Twice. Once to throw the first pitch after her University of Minnesota team made it to the Final Four, and again when she got a field pass during a Viking game.

"Both times are things I will never forget," she says now with a grin.

But the little girl who had imagined it didn't yet know of all that would happen before either event would take place.

The responsibility of being the oldest of five children was perhaps the very beginning. The technical skills required to be a great athlete would come, but it takes more than those to

 become a phenomenal sensation. Skills only go so far; a personal dedication to teamwork takes it the distance. Lindsay honed that aspect, along with her overall unassuming ways, at home growing up with her siblings.

There was Katie, four years younger, then Casey, born when Lindsay was six. Annie followed two years later, then Thomas, arriving when Lindsay was twelve. It was a full, active household geared for the activities of

young children where everyone pitched in to make it work. As the oldest, Lindsay took on her share by babysitting and doing general care, and credits her mother for seeing to it everything sailed along smoothly.

"My mom's the greatest," says Lindsay. "I know a lot of people say they have the best mom in the world, but I really do not know what I would do without my mom. I talk to her every day either by phone or e-mail now. When I was young, she was always there for us. I remember her always having snacks ready for us after school. During the winter she would make us all oatmeal or cream of wheat. That was the best! She took us around to our different sports and activities in our family mini-van. She always made sure we were taken care of and had what we needed."

Whether it was a warm winter breakfast or a ride in the van, Kathy Whalen saw to it that her children had what they needed throughout the year. But she also assigned them chores, not so much out of necessity as to give them the opportunity to develop a sense of responsibility. She protected and nurtured her children, and she also listened to each of them, honoring their individuality, and did her best to promote it—though when it came to Lindsay, it was not always an easy task.

"As a young mom, I was always worried that Lindsay wasn't trying enough different activities, but she knew her mind and knew what she enjoyed. Just sports. I enrolled her in a few, like gymnastics and figure skating, but she didn't much like those. What she wanted was a sport with a team. She'd practice alone, that wasn't problem, but that's all she liked. Team sports."

With a smile, Kathy tells of a very young Lindsay playing football by herself in the backyard, throwing the ball a ways out and then running to catch it herself, in the days before the younger ones were old enough to play with her. That practice proved useful when Lindsay joined a flag football team—the only girl to do so, but it got her on the team.

Lindsay on the ice.

Meanwhile, she had already begun playing hockey after going with her father, the coach, and watching him referee. He says, "The rink became her second home when she was just five or six. She would come to the games and watch me. She told me one time that people would sometimes swear and use my name, so I moved her down to the penalty box—a bit more out of range. She had her hot chocolate and a hot dog and maybe a box of Hot Tamales and she was set. She almost immediately wanted to play, and had a little bit of figure skating under her belt, so I decided she could give it a try. She'd be ready half an hour before it was time to go, and she always made sure she had five things in her bag—two skates, a helmet, and two gloves. She was so committed and determined, by the end of the week she was either first or second in all the drills."

It was a boys' team except for her, of which she generously says, "Not all of them treated me too great." At least not until she convinced them she could measure up to their standards. Once that happened—and it only took a week!—she became a full-fledged member of the team. Being an accepted member meant equal treatment, and, even though it wasn't a checking team, a player hit her once; she promptly smacked him back—an action that got her a strong reprimand from her father, making it a good lesson for everyone involved.

She stayed with hockey through fifth grade, at which point, at her parents' urging, she dropped that sport and moved on to basketball. There wasn't a varsity hockey team, and if she'd stayed where she was she'd have been in a checking league in sixth grade. The boys were getting too big. Thanks to her best friend Emily Inglis, whose father was the basketball coach, an alternative was waiting in the wings. It was a seemingly simple shift to a sport that would prove to be her forte—and one that had the same team element she found so appealing in hockey.

"I invited her to her first tournament when we were in elementary school," Emily says, of urging Lindsay to join. "She was playing hockey at the time, and we were short on players. Her first time down the floor, she made a left-handed reverse lay-up from the right side."

Her years playing hockey, Lindsay believes, helped her to deal with basketball's fast transitions, remain on guard, and keep an eye on the ball—and the other players—at all times. The rest, as we know, is raw talent.

Lindsay and Kelly Brinkman at Rothberg Basketball Camp.

Whatever the factors may have been, Lindsay took to basketball like a fish to water. "In 5th grade I played both hockey and basketball," she recalls. "I remember a lot about the first basketball game I ever played. It was in Litchfield in what I think is now their old high school gym. They since have built a new school there. The first shot I ever made in a game was from behind the backboard. I drove to the right and kind of got caught behind the board so I just took the shot anyway and it went up and over the backboard and went in. Running back down the court after that play I knew that I could play and this was a great, great game. We went on to win the game and I remember from that point on always wanting to play the game and be involved with a team.

"When I was in 7th grade," Lindsay continues, "my best friend Em and I got moved up to the 9th grade team, so of course we were the two smallest players on the team. When it came time to pick numbers I was the last one who got to choose because I was the youngest and the smallest, so I was "stuck" with the number 13. That number has stuck with me ever since, and I could not imagine having played high school, college, and WNBA in another jersey number. The only exception has been overseas where I'm number 7."

Those periods were still light years away, but the seed had been planted and it was taking root very quickly.

Emily adds, "There was a group of us that went to a number of youth basketball camps together. Most of us were content on impressing the coaches with fundamentals that had been taught throughout the week. I will always remember the expressions on the faces of those coaches as a twelve-year-old girl nailed no look passes and finished a finger-roll after being fouled by at least one defender; not a skill they had remembered addressing."

Lindsay was a natural. She was also picking up tennis at the time, but basketball remained in the forefront. She began taking a deeper interest in all aspects of the sport, making up her own brackets when it came to the NCAA playoffs, filling them out and hanging them on her bedroom walls. Her favorite professional team back then was the Phoenix Sun, and she had all the gear—the jacket, the hat, the shorts, and even a Sun backpack.

That's not to say she relinquished her fascination with her beloved Vikings and Twins. She was just adding to her stockpile of enthusiasms. But in one important respect, basketball was different. It was a sport she could actually play, and evidently play pretty well. That very feature gave it a kind of fun and challenge and stretch and promise she hadn't previously encountered in her young life. At the time she wasn't fully aware of its potential, however. All she knew was that she liked it even more than hockey.

"I really truly believe that a big reason why I have made it to where I am in basketball is my dad, and not just from hockey. Most of my skills come from playing sports with him all the time. Shooting baskets on the driveway, running football routes, playing soccer, playing catch in the backyard when he wasn't at work. I couldn't have asked for a better dad than him all the way around."

That tight-knit, active relationship extended from the hockey years as a grade-schooler through college, with such practice routines accepted as normal in the household. Sundays were a day of rest … at least until after church, that is.

"Before the Minnesota Vikings games—my favorite sports team ever—we had our hot sauce ready, along with chips and other dips that my mom would make. At halftime my dad and I would go out and play catch and work on routes to run. It was a total production every game. And we were so into it. If the Vikings lost, the rest of our day was ruined! It would take both of us a few days to recover."

To Lindsay's dad Neil, that interest in sports came naturally. He had played football and run track in high school, and was undefeated in wrestling until the 9th grade, when, forced to choose, he gave up the sport in favor of hockey. In hockey, he played goalie, was named an All-American and All-Conference player, and helped his team to three North

The Whalen kids: Casey, Katie, Lindsay, Annie, and Thomas.

Dakota Sate Championship titles.

Lindsay's admiration and respect for her father extends well past their sports connection and what he's done for her. She's watched him over the years provide for his family through shift work at 3M.

"I worked at 3M for three months during the summer before my freshman year at the U of M," she says. "So I got a taste of what it meant to work from 6 a.m. to 6 p.m. for three days and then turn around and work 6 p.m. to 6 a.m. a few days later. My dad has done that for our family for almost thirty years. I think that shows that he has always put our family first and done whatever it took for us to have the things we needed."

Lindsay's mom has also worked since shortly after the birth of her youngest child Thomas, making it necessary for Lindsay to help out at home between her own activities. Lindsay is amazed at how both her parents found not only the time but the energy to do all they've done for their children. She's thankful for having had the chance to do what she could for the family in the way of babysitting and chores, and thinks that the things she and her siblings did to chip in further strengthened and united the family.

Much to Neil and Kathy's credit, all five of their children are individuals with specific personalities, not easy to foster in a family of that size. Each has his or her own area in which to excel, and each is encouraged to cultivate their talents within it. The four younger siblings learned the pros and cons in having a famous older sister, and they took to calling her "The Golden Child" occasionally, due to the extra time their parents had to devote to Lindsay's schedule, but they accepted it and could not be more proud of her. They didn't always like being left waiting when autograph seekers clustered around her out in public, or being constantly asked if they were related when their last name was brought up, but they most certainly love Lindsay herself.

Katie, following closest behind Lindsay, took on the brunt of the cons. In junior high she too went out for basketball but the constant comparisons and expectations were a bit unnerving, and she eventually turned her attention exclusively to tennis and track. And friends. She's always had an outgoing personality and was just fine with the way it all fit for her. The remarkable bond she shares with Lindsay stems from the early days when the sisters shared a room, complete with gab sessions and goofing around when they were supposed to be trying to sleep.

"We would play tic-tac-toe on each other's backs," Katie says, "and then the person whose back was being played on had to guess the winner. Or we'd write out words the same way and the person had to then guess the word. Good memories."

As adults, they now meet for dinner as often as they can, which is a lot, Lindsay says, now that they live so close, and do plenty of that old gabbing by phone. Gone are the days of tic-tac- toe, Mario Brothers, Nintendo, and fighting over who gets the biggest cookie, but what has replaced them is just as nice.

Casey, next in line, has a mix of Katie's outgoing spirit and the family's love of sports and laughter. "Casey is one of the funniest people to be around," Lindsay says of him. "On Christmas morning, when we opened presents, we always looked forward to Casey's turn, because no matter what there was inside, you would have thought it was the best thing he'd ever seen. He just had genuine excitement and enthusiasm about every gift, and more importantly, who was giving it to him. When we were kids, Casey and I played every sport you could think of in our basement and backyard."

Annie is an avid reader and gifted artist, the only one of the bunch to enjoy just a dabbling of sports. She and Lindsay share the same taste in movies and have become very close as time has passed and the years between them have grown less significant. The same has happened with Thomas, the family baby, who currently plays football, basketball, and tennis, along with being an avid golfer. He also matches Lindsay wit for wit, having the same ultra-dry sense of humor they both inherited from their dad. Annie and Thomas were still quite young when Lindsay moved on to college, but the good times they had in the early days are well remembered and led to loving bonds as they grew.

Those good times in the beginning, especially when Lindsay helped with the babysitting, are also well-documented on tape. "Our dad had this giant VHS tape recorder," Katie recalls. "Lindsay would be the host, I was usually the camera-woman, and Casey was in the videos with Lindsay. We'd shoot pretend scenes, like at a restaurant where Lindsay was the owner/server and Casey was a guest "eating" with Annie or Thomas, who were 4 and 2 at the time. Or we would shoot a talk show with Lindsay as the host and Casey the guest, talking about some fake problem. Both scenarios usually ended up in some sort of mock fight where something ridiculous, like a ball accidentally hitting her square in the face, made Lindsay and Casey end up fake wrestling. One time she and Casey stuffed their clothes with pillows and did a mock sumo match, and Annie and Thomas, who were little at the time, insisted on having theirs stuffed too. We would spend hours making these videos in the basement, dressing up in all sorts of costumes, then show them to our parents. Those videos were hilarious at the time and get funnier every time we watch them."

That playful side of Lindsay still lurks behind the reserve of her public persona, even today. Yet the bits of it that do emerge, keenly honed to a dry edge, also contribute to her enormous appeal.

To the extent that weather allowed in their Midwestern town of hot summer days and cold winters, the play was outside rather than in the basement. It was not unusual to see the Whalen driveway—a slanted, gravel one at that—being used for anything and everything except parking. Neighborhood friends would join the Whalen kids to shoot hoops, play 2 on 2, 3 on 3, animated rounds of H-O-R-S-E or P-I-G, and sometimes with Lindsay and her insatiable appetite for practicing, merely 1 on 1 or, if need be (and Lindsay never minded), simply a concentrated game of 1-on-none.

When weather didn't permit, there was the challenge of indoor foosball or ping pong at home, though as often as not Lindsay would head off to the local school gym to shoot hoops for hours at a time from every conceivable angle and distance. There would be a pick-up game from time to time, but she was also quite content to practice alone. The long hours earned her the label of "gym rat" which has remained with her to this day.

During those days she was also picking up facts and stats on players in a range of sports, ever on a quest to learn. It was what interested her. Her Aunt Mary remembers the days of taking Lindsay to games and being amazed at her young niece's wealth of knowledge.

"I never had to worry about bringing the sports page, she knew all the facts about the Vikings and honestly about all the other teams," says Mary with a grin. But Mary wasn't simply impressed by that. She and other extended family members, a family with several good athletes amongst them, were also amazed at Lindsay's playing abilities. "At family gatherings, basketball games were common and she would overpower everyone even when she was quite young.

The sports were one thing; Lindsay's maturity, even as

Tubing on Lake Lizzie.

a youngster, was another. Family members attribute that maturity, in part, to the fact she was an only grandchild for four years in Neil's large family of eight siblings as well as Kathy's of five. Little Lindsay became the target of a great deal of their fun-loving ways, with various uncles and aunts buying her loud noise-making toys at Christmas and birth-days, perhaps just to irritate her parents. But it also had to do with early signs that Lindsay was game for anything.

"Her uncle Brian once told her to run her hands through her hair," tells Kathy. "During a meal, no less. Of course her hands were sticky gooey and everyone saw what was coming and laughed, but she did as she was told. She was so little but she ended up laughing right along with us."

Those holidays with the extended family were held in Grand Forks, North Dakota, where Neil and Kathy had grown up as high school sweethearts. As their brood grew in number, they continued to make the trip back home several times a year, piling everyone into their minivan. Katie was prone to carsickness so she always rode up front, putting Kathy in back to alternate with Lindsay feeding a baby or rocking another to sleep. Lindsay generally never minded being partial care taker. She took it on with the kind of pride that prompted her, when Thomas was born, to take the newborn to school for show-and-tell.

The family moved a year after Thomas's birth to a bigger house in another part of town. It had a smaller back yard and far fewer neighbor kids, much to Katie's dismay, but it also had a smooth, paved driveway with a sturdy hoop above it that pleased thirteen-year-old Lindsay. She practiced her shooting in that driveway from dawn until dusk on days when she could.

Basketball had become Lindsay's main focus by that time, though she still played tennis and was considering track. All the while, she kept tabs religiously on her favorite pro teams, including that of her first love, hockey.

"When I was about ten, my uncle Dan won tickets to game four the year the North Stars made it to the Stanley Cup Finals. They were front row seats! We lost that year to Pittsburgh but just getting to go to a game was great. Then, a few years later, Norm Green moved the team to Dallas and pro hockey was gone from Minnesota. I was so bummed when they moved. I think most of Minnesota was as well. Mike Modano is my all-time favorite hockey player!"

Lindsay knew her pro sports, and even today tries to keep up with them despite her own busy schedule. As the years passed and she became a professional herself, Lindsay's never lost track of her favorite pro teams. She's also never lost who she is. She is the same unassuming, funny, thoughtful person she was as a child, driven yet magnanimous along the way. The fairness she so eloquently displays on the court, a huge part of her popularity with fans, has always existed in all aspects of her life.

Her grandfather Whalen eloquently sums up that quality. "Since she's been old enough to talk, Lindsay has had an uncanny knack for always saying the right thing and being very considerate of others. And as the saying goes, doesn't 'puff up her chest' while doing so, even now with all her accomplishments. That ability to take the high road is maybe the main ingredient in the mystique surrounding her. She will only reflect the upside of a given situation, perhaps at times seeming to leave open the question of what she really thinks. That is answered by her actions. Her actions back up her words so consistently, the question answers itself. So mystique yes, mystery, no. Lindsay is who she is through and through, and that is not up for change."

And Lindsay returns such admiration. As the years passed and her renown as a player grew, autograph seekers began to surround her, yet she continued to acknowledge the presence of all four of her devoted grandparents, and her whole family, chatting as long as time allowed. Such a support system, extending to uncles, aunts, friends, and neighbors, makes it easy to see why Lindsay has such inner confidence. It's the kind of support system she acknowledges isn't always valued by others her age, something she finds very sad, because to her it has meant the world.

Playing for Hutchinson High School, Whalen went up for a layup in her senior season against Holy Angels.

2

HUTCHINSON HIGH

Hutchinson High School for Lindsay meant more than boys, books, and dances. While she still had plenty of time for those things, her high school experience brought Lindsay (as it has brought more and more girls in recent years) fully into the sports outlet she craved. These high school years served as the foundation for her professional career.

Lindsay had a fan's love for everything about basketball. She was fascinated by the creativity it allowed in all angles of passing and shooting, and studied the plays of the professionals with an eye for how they maneuvered and thought so quickly on their feet. Watching them play, she came to discern how they were able to do whatever it took, feeding a teammate out beyond the three-point line, driving the lane, or going for the quick jumper if an opponent's defense began to sag. Making plays required reading and responding to any situation that might arise. There were no guaranteed formulas or sure-fire tricks. That lesson, combined with her naturally unselfish personality, produced a style that Lindsay would hone to near perfection in the course of time.

Lindsay continued to participate in other sports, including tennis and track. Anything athletic that presented a challenge was likely to peak her interest. Her enthusiasm for her favorite professional teams in football and baseball stayed as strong as ever and she kept up with them all while focusing on her own primary goal. Posters hung on her bedroom wall of Charles Barkley, Jennifer Capriati, Kirby Puckett, and Anthony Carter, her chosen heroes and role models—though she spent far less time there than at the gym, where she could actually practice her shots and play.

Tennis ran a distant second to basketball during her high school years. It helped to keep her in shape, and she loved the challenges it presented as well as the team camaraderie. It also was pure fun, and although she worked hard to win, the recruitment pressures that she had begun to feel during the basketball season were pleasantly absent, and she loved the team bonding that took place over one mom's lasagna, another's pizza, on night's before a road trip in the coach's minivan to a match. Tennis gave her what she craved in terms of athleticism, teamwork, and relaxed yet exciting entertainment with friends.

She was also very, very good at it. A neighbor, attorney Ron McGraw, recalls, "The coach back then asked if my brother Mark and I would play doubles against Lindsay and her partner because she was such a good athlete and needed some competition. I don't recall the result of that match, but I assume Mark and I won at that point. It was probably the last time we could beat her at something. You could immediately tell that she not only had athletic ability, but she had what I call 'ice in her veins' instead of blood. She wanted to win in her quiet way, even in tennis. I told her a number of times, as her career developed, that I thought she ought to think about tennis as a life career because of her mental toughness and her athletic ability. I told her that I thought she could make more money playing tennis than basketball. Obviously I wasn't right on that, but it was always one of my thoughts."

Life away from tennis and basketball was as full as any girl's at that age, simply made fuller with those additions.

Lindsay at her grandparents' lake cabin in Bemidji.

She loved the water and spent a good share of the summer at either Emily's family cottage, a ten minute drive from town, or at her grandparents' lake cabin in Bemidji. There the family would take the pontoon out onto the lake and all the kids would jump off and swim. Tubing and jet skis also captured her interest, though her Grandparents Vilandre remember her still unable to resist the hoop even on vacation.

"Everyone else would be in or on the water but Lindsay would be out in the backyard, where we had a basketball net installed on the driveway, shooting hoops. A good friend of ours who has played, coached, scouted, and managed hockey teams his whole life challenged her to a game of HORSE. She demolished him in short order, much to his amazement—and enjoyment."

Lindsay was thoroughly enjoying herself as she built her budding career in basketball. She had a group of close friends who regularly went to school football games together. On weekends they would pile at someone's house with sleeping bags to watch movies, and occasionally, when at Lindsay's, drag out the old video camera and shoot skits or reenact scenes from *Day of Our Lives*, complete with misquoted lines and more than a few made-up scenarios. The group didn't share Lindsay's devotion to sports, although some were into volleyball, but they all had plenty of interests in common. They have stayed connected from those teen years to the present, a wonderful tribute to the strength and beauty of true friendship.

Along with friends, family, tennis and basketball, Lindsay also found time to run track. Through it was a rather short lived phase in the context of her overall career, within its span Lindsay showed her first true colors as a player. Her Aunt Mary recalls watching as the end of a relay neared and a runner on Lindsay's team dropped the baton. It cost the team the race. Immediately afterwards Lindsay ran to the girl to console her. Mistakes happen, Mary overheard her say. A thoughtful, generous act, and a sign of Lindsay's blossoming athletic spirit.

Later in that 10th grade year, while running a 4x100 relay, the tables turned and it was Lindsay who fell within meters of the finish line, undermining her team's chances of going to the state tournament. Although she felt bad about flailing into another runner, the ungraceful fall would have made for good You Tube, she says, if You Tube had existed back then. But the consequences of the fall weren't funny in the least. Lindsay felt her hip pop when she hit the ground and had to be carried off the field. An x-ray revealed that she'd badly torn a hip flexor muscle. With no trainer or rehab at that time, she did as she was told and didn't run for two months. That wasn't a problem since walking alone was a bit painful and the best she could do was limp. The accident also gave her a deep cut on her knee—the scar is still visible. She was happy she'd already attended prom, but her slow recovery made for a few long summer months of tedium and cut her basketball practice short for the upcoming year.

By that fall, basketball was beginning to be a preoccupation. She still ran around with her group of friends and attended prom again that year, but between basketball practice and games, her passion for the sport was becoming almost all-consuming. She was good. She knew it. She'd never liked anything so much in her life. It was the smell of the gym, the feel of the ball, the way each play pushed her to new levels of passing or shooting. She loved the structure, the plays, the game. And a few recruiters, in turn, were taking serious notice.

The seed planted when she and Emily had been kids playing hoops for fun had definitely taken firm hold. Emily, who was also on the high school team with her, says now, "It's hard to say exactly how she has achieved so many goals that are simply aspirations for most, because she works hard quietly. Not only does she have an obviously natural talent, but she also loves what she does, and I'm not quite sure which came first. As kids, she was typically the last one in the group that would want to go inside whether we were playing basketball, soccer, or any number of full contact games. We used to sign little pieces of paper and exchange them saying, 'Keep this; it's going to be worth something some day.' I think that was the last time I signed an autograph." For Lindsay, it was just the beginning, and may have been a premonition of things yet to come.

It would have been a big dream for a young girl in those days, since the Women's National Basketball Association (counterpart of the NBA) didn't exist at the time. (The Women's Professional Basketball League was by then a distant memory. It had struggled from 1978 to 1981, with the Minnesota Fillies as the local team.) The WNBA was founded in 1996 and had its first game a year later. Lindsay was in high school by then.

She admits it's strange to think how young the sport is at the professional level and is grateful that it's thriving, not only for the sake of her own career, but for the opportunities it offers to fans and other players.

"Everyone deserves the chance to have a professional life in sports, man or woman, if that's what they choose and work hard to obtain."

And work hard she did. In her junior year she joined the Amateur Athletic Union (AAU) and traveled for summer camp, both out of love of the game and to improve her play, should a basketball career turn out to be in the cards for her. The advent of the WNBA was making that a distinct possibility. Under Hutchinson High Coach Andy Rostberg's direction, she was beginning to refine her technique and become more comfortable on the court with the skills she already possessed.

Ron McGraw was a fan of the game and followed her development throughout those early years. "I watched Lindsay play all through her high school days, both home and away. My wife asked me one day why in the world I was watching girls' basketball more, or at least equal to the amount of time I spent watching boys' basketball. I told her that Lindsay Whalen could do things that I hadn't seen boys do in a basketball court. She was unbelievably good at being a team leader, a play maker, and making others really look good, as opposed to trying to make herself look good. Of course the result was that she looked good too, because she could do so many things. Besides her talent, she has a way of using her cute little smile when playing against someone, and

The Hutchinson High School team: Lindsay is second from the left.

the next thing the player knows she's just been beaten about six different ways."

The McGraws' granddaughters also became fans of Lindsay's play, and during her college career they passed their enthusiasm on to their friends. Lindsay didn't yet know it at the time, but the inspiring example she was setting for the McGraw granddaughters and other fans would later become a career ambition—showing the next generation that anything is possible.

As a junior Lindsay averaged 22.8 points, 5.8 rebounds, and 4.3 assists. In her senior year she suffered her first sprained left ankle but it didn't keep her off the floor for long. Lindsay was gaining stride. In addition to her hotshot passing and ability to score, she was learning how to lead without theatrically taking charge on the floor, and how to watch the movement all around her with an eagle eye while bringing the ball up the court. What would become eventually her legendary unselfishness in play took hold on the court in that gym.

She would be amply rewarded for it. By the end of her senior year, along with having been an All-conference selection in track and tennis, she'd led the Hutchinson team to three consecutive Minnesota Conference basketball championships and was herself a four-time All-Missota Conference pick.

Though Coach Rostberg was ecstatic with the team wins and her play, Lindsay admits that she gave him a few gray hairs along the way. "One of my favorite plays was against undefeated New Prague. There were two minutes to go and we were up by four, and I knew it was risky but I came down on a break and found a post player so did a behind-the-back pass. It'd have been safer, I know, to hold the ball but the crowd apparently liked it and we won."

The zeal behind her spirited risks and the attitude that "the worst thing that can happen is you get yelled at and taken out of the game for a minute" is what fans love about her, and coaches, despite turning gray, depend on to win games. She plays fearlessly and pushes the boundaries of what can be done on the court, both for her own growth and to contribute to the creative play of the game.

Her sister Katie puts it best: "She has really truly worked hard from day one. She was blessed with a talent but made the most of it by dedicating herself to becoming the best that she could be. She spent many hours in the winter, chipping away ice on the driveway so that she could play. She spent hours alone in the gym practicing free-throws. She didn't let

Lindsay's senior picture.

anything stop her; she kept playing and doing what she loved because it made HER happy."

It's that honest drive simply to do what she loves as well as she can that has propelled Lindsay to extraordinary heights. High school was the beginning. Her efforts there earned her a full university scholarship—a blessing for her parents, who had four other children yet to help put through college.

Lindsay ended her high school years as the school's all-time points leader with 1996, along with an impressive 556 rebounds and 575 assists. Many of her records still stand today. She's the only Hutchinson athlete to have the honor of having her number retired, and in 2008 was inducted into the Hutchinson High School Hall of Fame as outstanding graduate.

Also honored in the Hall of Fame was Ron McGraw, noted in part for his pioneering efforts to bring attention to the women's basketball program, which in Lindsay's day was still in its infancy. For all of her accomplishments, during her high school years Lindsay had gone virtually unnoticed by many Hutchinson residents, simply because the sport didn't have a high profile. However, times are changing and the growing popularity of women's basketball in general is a gift for all the fans who have learned to enjoy it, not to mention the players who are being given the opportunity to follow in Lindsay's footsteps.

Joel Niemeyer, Sports Director and Assistant Program Coordinator at KDUZ/KARP Radio in Hutchinson, has seen exactly that. "The impact that Lindsay Whalen had on young girls in Minnesota can be seen on high school basketball courts all over the state. The quality of play in girls' high school basketball has improved dramatically because so many kids want to be like Lindsay."

Lindsay, in doing what she loved and doing it with everything in her, left a bigger mark than anyone at that time could have imagined, including Lindsay herself.

Lindsay kept her #13 during her four years with the Gophers.

3

A GOLDEN GOPHER

What the basketball program at the University of Minnesota did for Lindsay is equal to what Lindsay did for the sport. She brought her skills to a professional level during her years with the Gophers and came out a seasoned player, widely sought after by professional teams hoping to become contenders. In exchange, in her senior year, Lindsay led the Golden Gophers to their first-ever Final Four appearance.

When she began her four years at Minnesota in 2000, an average Gopher game might draw a thousand fans. As a women's sport, it just didn't garner the same amount of attention as the men's team did. With her unique style of executing plays, Lindsay changed all that. Attendance began growing, and by her senior year it had increased tenfold. Put in the best and simplest terms, Lindsay was fun to watch. By 2004, she had brought about a remarkable renaissance in the University of Minnesota's women's basketball program, the only Division I school in the state. The turnaround was so dramatic, in fact, the team moved permanently from the

Sports Pavilion to the much larger Williams Arena after her first year on the team.

Her choice of the U of M over other schools came rather easily to the Minnesota native who so honors her roots, lending some truth to the urban legend that Lindsay had turned down an offer from the University of Iowa Hawkeyes because they didn't broadcast Viking games in the region. Although not heavily recruited out of Hutchinson High, it still was not a difficult choice. Lucky for the Gophers! She would turn them from a "cellar dweller" team with seven straight losing seasons to a three-time NCAA tournament qualifier, capped by a spectacular Final Four run, and bring the program's million-dollar financial deficit within sight of turning a profit.

None of these accomplishments were in the forefront of Lindsay's thoughts when she signed on with the Gophers. At 5' 9", she was rather short by women's basketball standards, and she just wanted a chance to play ball. And play she did. Averaging 20.3 points per game, she finished her career with 2,285 points—the most scored by any player, male or female, in U of M history. That's playing.

During her freshman year Lindsay remained under the radar for the most part, primarily because the team wasn't winning much; they posted a less-than-stellar 8-20 season that year, and fans weren't flocking to the games. But by the time she appeared in her first Big Ten game on January 4, 2001 (which resulted in a tie with Indiana) Lindsay had already made a strong impression on dedicated fans like Sue Corbin.

"As a loyal Gopher women's basketball fan since the early 80s," says Sue, past president of the Minnesota Fast Break Club, the booster organization for Gopher women's basketball, "I have to admit, I wasn't very optimistic about the 2000–2001 season, until I went to the first exhibition game that fall and got my first glimpse of #13. It was clear she was something special. In fact, during games at the Pav with the small crowds, you could often hear everything the coaches were saying in the huddle. Often as not, Coach Littlejohn would direct her comments to Lindsay, with the usual gist being, 'Lindsay, create something out there'."

If only there'd been more such fans. Lindsay, so excited to be playing, recalls that same quiet from the floor, the echo of the team grunts, the squeak beneath their feet, the hollow thumping of the ball as every sound bounced off empty seats and vacant walls. She hadn't really known what to expect, but never imagined it would be like this.

Still, she was playing. The players began adapting to each other and developing a style, and by the next year they began to win, with Lindsay leading the way. She personally nabbed five Big Ten Player of the Week awards in 2002, and that year the team as a whole pulled off the biggest team turnaround in women's Big Ten history.

Meanwhile, the fans they did have were beginning to spread the word. Crowd size doubled, tripled, quadrupled, with everyone coming to cheer on the team and to watch this player who fought with every fiber of her being for a loose ball, who could spin on a dime and put that same spin into the ball with dead-perfect aim at the hoop, or, no less often,

"She can be graceful and fleeting..."

pass it off to a teammate in a better position to score. In her sophomore year Lindsay averaged 22.8 points, 6 assists, and 2.4 steals a game, reaching 1000 career points in only 51 games. That's who the fans were coming to see.

"As a person who covered the team," KSTP's Joe Schmit

recalls, "I was not only amazed at her talent, but at her toughness. I saw her get bulled over on a charge, help the player up who hit her. She then told the opponent, 'Don't ever do that again or I will mess you up.' You did not want to mess with Lindsay."

Such unabashed aggression and masterful flair, accompanied by what seemed like a contradictory shyness, created an intriguing persona that fed Lindsay's growing stature as a sports celebrity. Fans wanted to have an autograph, to pose for a photo; media wanted interviews. And everyone seemed to want a peak into the elusive person who, once off the floor, had such a fascinating reserve.

That aspect of the game—the part that required more than playing ball—didn't come easily to Lindsay. It just wasn't in her nature to open up to even the most well-meaning and appreciative strangers. She has gradually learned to accept that part of her career as well, seeing it as an honor and an opportunity—a platform to spread encouragement about women's sports. She's actually become quite proficient at it but will never completely relish it. She'd rather just be playing ball.

The basketball court, the game itself, is Lindsay Whalen's comfort zone. That's where she's at home. That's where she displays an art that only comes from determined use of natural talent. Descriptions of her style run the gamut of superlatives. She can be graceful and fleeting, seemingly moving on air and keeping both the crowd and other players in the dark, wondering from second to second just what she'll do next. Her confidence on the floor more than compensates for her shyness off of it. Lindsay knows what she's doing. Her teammates know she knows, and they wait with as much readiness as possible. There's no way to tell when a lightning behind-the-back pass may strike Lindsay as the right move, or when she'll decide to just throw.

Her college roommate and fellow Golden Gopher Kim Danlo (formerly Kim Nelson) remembers very well what being on the court with Lindsay was like. "I gave up counting the number of times Lindsay would hit someone in the face or stomach with the ball during practice. We actually had to run drills that would help everyone keep their hands up and be ready for her passes."

She did it in the name of winning. But while she led the team, as was her duty as point guard, she also quickly became known as the team's most unselfish player, constantly alert to make sure the ball got to whomever was best situated to make the shot, without being shy about taking it herself if, in the split-second moment of decision, that seemed like the best thing to do.

Lindsay was named the Big Ten Women's Player of the Year for those efforts in 2001—only the fourth sophomore ever to receive that honor. That year she also became the only player in Big Ten history to be named Player of the Week five times in one season—a season that gave the team a shining 22-8 record and took them to the second round in the NCAA Division 1 tournament.

But life wasn't all basketball. Lindsay kept up her studies in pursuit of a sports management degree. Though time spent at classes, study, practice, and games didn't leave much

Kim Nelson, Lindsay, and Lindsay Lieser.

for social activities, she squeezed in time for a new guy named Ben Greve, and began what would become a lifelong relationship. Their personalities clicked from the start. Ben quickly caught on to her jokester ways, learning as her friends had that Lindsay never takes life too seriously.

"One day Linds and I were eating cereal before we left for class," remembers roommate Kim. "Above our cupboards and below the ceiling was extra space. We kept our cereal boxes there. We started wondering if we could get up there and fit in between the cupboards and the ceiling. Lindsay decided she wanted to find out. She carefully climbed above the sink, pulled herself up above the cupboards, and squeezed in below the ceiling. Sure enough, she fit! It was a funny sight with her all cramped up in this little space. I told her not to move because I wanted to take a picture. As I went to my room to search for the camera, our new roommate happened to walk in the door. We had just met her the week before. She walked right by Linds in the kitchen and didn't even see her, but came back to the kitchen a minute later and opened the fridge. Linds didn't know what to do so she made this funny noise and completely surprised our roommate. The timing of it all was hilarious!"

They also devised a game they called Cash Cow where one would stand on the kitchen countertop with handfuls of coins, bills, a watch, anything of value, and the other would run down the short hall to the computer room and cranked out a tune—usually something by Outkast when it was Lindsay's run. The tune was a signal for whoever was up on the countertop to drop the stash and see how much the other could run back and grab before it hit the floor.

"Everyone knows Linds is a hustler on the court," Kim adds. "But they haven't seen anything until they've seen her play Cash Cow."

A competitor through and through.

She brought that same spirit to basketball as a junior, in a season that saw the third new coach in three years enter the picture. While Cheryl Littlejohn didn't leave of her own accord (she was let go for various rule violations) Lindsay's second-season coach, Brenda Oldfield, fresh into coaching, opted to further her new career at the University of Maryland after one year in Minnesota. The opening left room for the entrance of Coach Pam Borton.

Of playing under different coaching styles, Lindsay is nonchalant. "It's a good way to better our plays. Every coach has a different style. Learning how to adjust gives us an advantage."

All the same, before the team could experience the glories of what Coach Borton would bring, they had to deal with the sad and shocking departure of Coach Oldfield. Lindsay got to work phoning new recruits to reassure them the coaching change wouldn't upset plans for a great season ahead. She did what she could to ease the transition, working to ameliorate the effects of the change and create the best environment for the upcoming year.

Coach Oldfield's style had helped bring the team to a 22-8 record in 2001 and the second round of the NCAA tournament; that year she was named AP Coach of the Year. Coach Borton knew she faced a challenge in agreeing to coach a talented organization that had already been shifted from technique to technique, and had developed a special brand of stick-together and win-regardless chemistry with Lindsay anchoring the team. Nevertheless she began her work, emphasizing a strong defensive game geared more toward one-on-one strategy than zone play. Much of it was new and sometimes challenging to Lindsay but, as she had predicted, under Coach Borton's guidance she learned and became a better player. Her concentration on other players' moves became so acute it was almost as if she was orchestrating the outcome before it happened.

Despite wearing a permanent scowl on her face, a result of intense concentration, Lindsay moved as if on automatic, making the sport seem so easy anyone could do the same. Her style of play, both on offense and defense, was fascinating to watch, and as word got around the fan base grew, extending even to sports enthusiasts who had never before taken a women's sport seriously. Those who succumbed to their curiosity and bought a ticket were likely to witness an exhibit of exceptional skill and teamwork. Lindsay would dazzle, as would 6'2" center Janel McCarville, while the rest of the team, both individually and as a unit, added further strength and split-second coordination to round out the show.

Terry McFarland, who passed away in February 2010, was former president of the Fast Break Club and one of the team's biggest fans. He hadn't thought women's sports could hold a candle to men's when it came to athleticism or entertainment until he first saw Lindsay play the sport with such precision and skill during the 2000–2001 season. By the time Janel joined the team the next year he was hooked, and he wasn't the only one. Above and beyond the student base, men and women of all ages, including one ninety-two-year-old who heard about Lindsay and came to see what all the fuss was about, had begun to show up in large numbers. Attendance set an all time high in January of 2003, when more than 13,000 fans showed up to watch the team beat Big Ten defending champions Purdue. The women's Golden

Gophers had built a strong team and a strong reputation and they were now putting on a show that left few disappointed.

They were also winning. They ended the 2002–2003 season with a 25-6 record—12-4 conference and 13-2 non-conference. This record earned them a berth in the NCAA tournament where they reached the semi-finals before falling to Texas. That year Lindsay received more post-season awards than ever, being chosen as team MVP and selected unanimously to the All-Big Ten first team. She was also selected for the Big Ten Conference All-Academic Team with a 3.42 GPA. And to top things off, she was immortalized in a Lindsay bobblehead—a first for any U of M athlete.

In July, Lindsay traveled to Croatia as a member of the U.S. team to compete at the FIBA World Championship for Young Women. They won the gold medal, and the experience was enriching—tiring, yet invigorating. But before long Lindsay was once again getting ready for a Gopher season she hoped would take them all the way to the top.

She wasn't the only one. Coming into the 2003–2004 season, tickets for the women's games became difficult to get even through scalpers, but those lucky enough to have them were in for a fabulous ride. Not only was the team good, but many of the players—thirteen in all—were home-grown Minnesotans. Pride was running high. It was Lindsay, however, who drew the most attention. Coach Borton recalls some indicative signs:

WELCOME TO WHALENS WORLD

WHALEN FOR MAYOR

"LINDSAY WILL YOU MARRY ME"

(That from a preteen boy.)

HOT DOGS - $1

PARKING - $8

WATCHING LINDSAY PLAY – PRICELESS

There were stands selling Whalen bobbleheads, Whalen pins, and replica #13 jerseys, so many of which were already visible on young Twin Cities girls. Lindsay, tremendously appreciative for the fan support of her and of the team, kept her focus on getting the job at hand done.

"We're really so focused," she explained. "We're concentrating so hard on doing our best. It's like we all have a feeling this year we could do something for Minnesota, something that's never been done. It'd be great if in twenty years or so they look back and see that we started something good, that there were a lot of Final Fours and a few championships after us."

Amidst the pandemonium surrounding her, from fans to accolades, a sense of additional purpose was adding to Lindsay's love of the game. It had become clear she was having an impact on the younger generation, and on the growth of the fan base in general for women's basketball. Alongside her magic on the court, Lindsay's inspirational role would remain a meaningful and important aspect of her work in the years ahead.

She was already well-suited to be a role model, due to her unencumbered, nearly egoless personality. This sincere, ingenuous, girl-next-door quality, allied with her mesmerizing play, made her the kind of sports phenomenon that young players and fans would naturally idolize. She is private but never dismissive of anyone's questions; she's down to earth, polite—unless you're standing in her way on the court—and gracious, but not gushy. She accepts questionable ref calls as just part of the game. She's grounded firmly in who she is and what she does—nothing more, nothing less. She's instantly liked by all who meet her because she's completely transparent. What you see is who she is.

And as the 2003–2004 season unfolded, Lindsay was nothing less than spectacular. She would be the first to admit that her exploits were made possible only though the uncanny coordination of the team as a whole. She, Kadidja Andersson, Leslie Hill, and Lori Dimitroff had spent four years mastering their ability to play in sync. Dominating center Janel McCarville, a junior, had come on board with them for the past three, as had top reserve forward Tanisha Gilbert. Newcomers Kelly Roysland, Liz Podominick, and Jamie Broback combined with Christina Collison, Shannon Bolden, Hannah Garry, and Shannon Schonrock to complete a team who, in 2003–2004, had the most wins in a single season in U of M history.

Meanwhile Lindsay had managed to maintain a 3.23 GPA and a semblance of a social life, spiced very nicely by Ben. An aspiring pro athlete himself at the time, he understood the rigors of managing time during the course of an intense season of competition, but he wasn't about to let her get away due to any of that, nor was she tempted to leave.

Her final regular-season Big Ten game was on February 8, 2004, with home court advantage against fifth-ranked Penn State. The crowd at Williams Arena was a staggering 14,000 plus, and at one point, at the sight of Lindsay pulling out one of her breathtaking plays, the entire crowd rose in ovation.

Then, on February 12, in a game against Ohio State at their Value City Arena, with three minutes remaining in the first half, Lindsay fell to the floor and remained there clutching her right wrist. X-rays later revealed she'd fractured two metacarpal bones. She'd be out four to six weeks.

It was a devastating blow, but both Lindsay and the team carried on as best they could. She attended the games, her arm in a cast, and was honored with a halftime ceremonial tribute of [#]13. The number, so aimlessly chosen long before because its uniform fit, had also been made famous by another Gopher point guard, Deb Hunter, from 1979 to 1983. Hunter still holds school records in assists (632) and steals (413). The number had served each wearer well.

The injury put an end to Lindsay's run of 106 consecutive starts, and in all likelihood her career. It also dealt a blow to the team's winning streak. After that Ohio game, which ended in a 57-75 loss with Lindsay sitting out the second

Lindsay in a cast before the Iowa game, February 19, 2004.

half, the team continued on through a 4-3 streak. Their wins early in the season would help their contention standing, but the outlook for post-season success no longer looked as promising as it had at the onset of the year.

Then came the first NCAA round on March 21st against UCLA, vividly remembered by super-fan Sue Corbin. "The day of the first-round game, it still wasn't clear if Whalen would be playing, but when we came to the arena, she was suited up and on the court, albeit with a fairly large bandage on her shooting hand. Much to the delight of the fans, Lindsay was in the starting line-up, and within the first minute or so, she puts up a 3-pointer—swish, nothing but net. As she ran down court to get back on defense, she raised her bandaged hand to the crowd, as if to tell us.... the kid is back."

Lindsay remembers the gesture a bit differently, acknowledging that she only meant it to signal the next defense position, but the enthusiastic roar of the crowd was deafening in either case.

The Gophers won that night 92-81, with Lindsay scoring 31 points to lead the way for the Gophers. Nikki Blue led UCLA scorers. The following night they defeated Kansas State 80-61. It was in those two games, Sue thinks, "that the mystique of Lindsay Whalen was permanently etched in Maroon and Gold."

The team ended the regular season with a 25-9 record and Lindsay was again named team MVP. She'd averaged 20.5 points and 5.4 assists and had set a U of M individual scoring record (male or female) with 2285 career points.

Next step, the NCAA West Regionals. The women were back on their game and the energy, hopes, and ambitions were once again at an all-time high. They'd gotten this far before, only to have their hopes dashed in the opening rounds. This year was different. The whole team could feel it. Minnesota fans were holding their breath.

They took the first regional game against Boston College 76-63, and were set to face Duke for the regional championship that would give them the right to go on to the Final Four. The excitement level rose to fever pitch for fans all over Minnesota, although in Lindsay's hometown of Hutchinson it may have reached even higher.

"The Gophers were set to play Duke," says Joel Niemeyer, sports director for KDUZ in Hutchinson. "I was set to plop myself in my favorite chair and watch the game. It got to be tip-off time, and my wife, who was pregnant with our first child at that time, told me I had to go to the store for her. All dads and dads-to-be know better than to mess with a pregnant woman with a craving. So even though I knew I'd miss the first part of the game I went to the local grocery store to get her craving. Now this grocery store is probably the biggest grocery store in the area. Folks from the entire region make it a point to go there for their food. When I pulled into the lot I couldn't believe what I saw… four cars… mine would be the fifth. Outside of the stock boy and cashier, I think there were maybe three people in the store. Driving back to my place I noticed that no one was walking on the streets, no cars were parked on Main Street. It was like the entire town of Hutchinson had shut down for Lindsay's game. Only she could shut down a town of 13,000 plus. Course I guess we all had good reason to watch that game… and that 7-point win."

The Gopher women's team defeated Duke by a score of 82 to 75 that night, thus securing a place in the NCAA Final Four for the first time in the school's history.

The team arrived home to a waiting crowd of more than two hundred fans—a seemingly small turnout but actually rather large for 2 a.m. And for the Whalen family, who had attended the game against Duke in Virginia, well-wishers had cooked up a big surprise. In an effort to express their pride and excitement, they'd decorated the Whalen's entire house, inside and out: messages written on mirrors, streamers in the trees, chalked messages on their sidewalk.

"It was truly a mess," says Kathy. "But a fun mess."

Parents of the Gopher players before the Duke game, March 29, 2004.

The team departed again a few days later for the Final Four in New Orleans, where they were scheduled to face the Connecticut Huskies, and so did the Whalen clan, whose trip was funded almost entirely by other Hutchinson families so that all seven of them could go. The Whalens felt extremely grateful for such generosity and were also appreciative of kind neighbor Bridget Peller, who volunteered to clean up their house while they were away.

A close-knit group of nineteen, including other parents the Whalens had gotten to know during the past four exciting years, joined all the Minnesota fans who made the trek to witness this historic event. In true Minnesota fashion, they cheered and booed and held up signs for their heroes, urging their team on in any way they could. They watched with baited breath as the Huskies took an 11-point lead, which the Gophers cut to eight in the last few minutes at the half. Their deafening chants of "Believe" helped bring on a second-half

Gopher surge that saw the Huskies' lead drop to four and then to two. With just over 12 minutes remaining, the Huskies star, Diana Taurasi, reversed the momentum, sinking a fine 3-pointer. The Huskie's soon had a 9-point lead. The Gophers answered with seven points of their own, including a big 3-pointer by Jamie Broback, cutting the deficit to only two points with just under eight minutes to go. The score sat at 53-51. The Gophers stole the ball in the next three possessions and had good shots but no luck with net. The game went into a two-and-a-half minute scoreless stretch, finally broken by Huskie Ann Strother's 3-pointer. The Gophers fought back and got to within five points, not succumbing until the end, when the Huskies sank four out of four from the free throw line to seal the fate of the game.

Connecticut had won 67-58, and went on to defeat Tennessee 70-61 to secure the NCAA championship. Minnesota fans were tremendously disappointed, of course, but also very proud of the team that had entered the nation's elite and advanced to the cusp of a national championship.

Without Lindsay's contribution, the team is unlikely to have risen so high, yet she would be the first to acknowledge that the Gophers' success has always been a team endeavor. And what the Gopher women did as a team paved the way for the teams to follow, increasing both appreciation and expectations. Since then, Gopher women have continued to draw enough fans to be considered one of the most popular teams in the United States in their sport.

All the same, there is no use denying that from 2000 to 2004 Lindsay was the face of the team. She shouldered

Lindsay with her family, U of M Athletic Direcor Joel Maturi, and Goldy Gopher at a ceremony to retire her number.

that responsibility with an aplomb that had to be seen to be believed. During her years with the Gophers they moved into the top twenty nationally in attendance and have stayed there ever since. Those same fans who were initially drawn to Lindsay's superstar persona developed an appreciation of the team and the sport itself that have kept them coming back.

Lindsay was elected to the Hutchinson KDUZ Hall of Fame in 2004, becoming its youngest member. The young girls who attend Coach Borton's summer basketball Champ Camp often wear a #13 jersey in honor and memory of her achievements. The U of M began attracting top state and national recruits after what became known as the Whalen

Era. Lindsay has indeed left her mark on the U's women's basketball program, while, along with her teammates, bringing it to unprecedented levels of success on the court. They had accomplished the goal they'd set out to do. They'd made history.

The next step for her would be the college draft and a pro career in the Women's National Basketball Association. There is a tinge of irony, perhaps, in the fact that her final college match-up was against a team from Connecticut, for that state would soon play an even more important role in her career. But for the time being Lindsay was headed back home for a well-deserved break with her family and Ben.

Lindsay in defense mode in a game against the Lynx.

4

CONNECTICUT SUNSHINE

Connecticut Sun coach Mike Thibault had already made his decision when he watched her play in the fall of 2003, but he kept it to himself the best he could until the season's end, when the final standings gave the Suns the fourth pick in the first round, three better than Lindsay's home-state pro team, the Lynx. The Lynx did what they could to keep Lindsay in Minnesota by making a pre-draft trade that raised their pick to sixth, but it wasn't enough to top Coach Thibault; he didn't give them the chance.

Lindsay couldn't help but tell Coach Thibault that she was hoping to be drafted by her home-state team, to continue riding the wave of fan approval she'd built up over the past four years. Minnesota was home. She could accomplish so much more there. But she knew full well that the sport was also a business, and she made it clear she'd give her utmost to whatever team succeeded in drafting her.

Coach Thibault didn't spell it out at the time, but his experience as a coach had convinced him that aside from the benefits she'd bring to the Sun on the court, Lindsay would be better off starting her professional career in Connecticut. The pressure placed on any rookie was bad enough, without it coming with the force this particular rookie would have faced in Minnesota, where she was adored, revered to an overwhelming extent. No, Lindsay needed to hone her skills away from the intense scrutiny that such adoration would have placed on her.

Though Thibault knew he had a good point, he also knew it would take Lindsay a while to see it.

When the Sun drafted Lindsay as the fourth pick of the first round, it was the highest that any Big Ten player had ever been taken. (The next year her former Gopher teammate Janel McCarville would be drafted at [#]1.) The $40,800 salary that came with the draft gave Lindsay room to splurge a bit, on a video console—her very own.

The Connecticut Sun is owned by the Mohegan Indian tribe, the first WNBA franchise not owned by an NBA owner. Its home base is in the Mohegan Sun Casino, the second largest casino in the United States, with a 12,000-seat arena. The team, founded in 1999 in Florida and known then as the Orlando Miracle, moved to Connecticut in 2002 and became the Sun shortly before the 2003 WNBA season, the year before Lindsay joined them.

When she was picked Lindsay put on a brave face and struggled to muster an attitude of acceptance. The day after the draft, Coach Thibault and his wife Nancy invited her and her parents to come to Connecticut as a welcoming gesture and to put all minds at ease, putting them up for the night in the presidential suite of the casino and arranging a lovely dinner. Both Lindsay and her parents became instantly fond of their hosts' warmth and were awestruck at the facility.

"They really made me feel welcome. It seemed to be a great place," Lindsay said. "And for them to put us in that suite was so nice. The view was unbelievable, we could see for miles all around. Really spectacular."

That inaugural good-will trip made her a bit more relaxed when time came for the actual move, yet when she stepped off the plane by herself everything lying ahead was new. A new apartment, her first time living alone. New surroundings. Nothing was familiar, not the town, not the people. Coming from the clamor of constant and customary activity back home, it was all very strange.

Although she had a number of new fans anxious to see her play her first game with the Sun, no one yet waved in recognition when she walked down a street or shopped for groceries. No one asked for an autograph. Her first nights were spent quietly in her apartment, her days at practice with the team. At the time she had no idea who they were either … or that they would soon become such close friends.

She knew them by name from the start, that part wasn't hard. There were other rookies in the mix which helped, and the more seasoned players, like Katie Douglas, who was to become a lifelong friend, were great in helping the newbies adjust. Two games into the season, Lindsay was beginning to get her footing and she let loose with a bit more aggression, trying as point guard to lead a team she hadn't yet quite figured out. She also was letting more and more of her wily humor surface.

The team answered back with some of its own. In its first regular-season game, the home opener against Phoenix on May 22, 2004, the players agreed to run out all together for pre-game intros with Lindsay going first. The rest of the team had privately agreed to hold back at the entrance, and laughed hysterically as she ran her solo route across the court in embarrassment. Lindsay was getting as good as she gave.

Those pranks, and time, helped to make Lindsay feel more at home. She credited the seasoned pros on the team, Taj McWilliams-Franklin, Nykesha Sales, Brooke Wyckoff, and Katie Douglas, for serving as good examples to her and the other rookies on how to rise to a professional level. Even though they lost five of their first eight games, things looked encouraging.

Still, what many except the most ardent fans didn't realize, says Bill Tavares, Media Relations Director for the Sun, was what a precarious position Lindsay was in that first season. She, a rookie, was expected to lead as point guard a team of two noted veterans and All-Stars in Nykesha Sales and Taj McWilliams-Franklin, plus others with far more experience than she had. They'd just lost their four-time All-Star Shannon "Pee Wee" Johnson in the trade for Lindsay, and the logic escaped them in the beginning. Combine that with the fact many of the fans had wanted the team to draft Diana Taurasi, the Phoenix Mercury pick, although they realized there had been no way to get her. They were happy with Lindsay as a great consolation prize, and sent e-mails to the coach to prove it, yet between that and her rookie status on the team, Lindsay had a huge mountain to climb.

In June a bad case of strep throat knocked Lindsay for

a loop. She suffered through the worst of it and came back stronger and more determined than ever to pick up the momentum. Her assists rose from 3.3 to 5.7. One of Coach Thibault's goals was to have a team that shared the ball, and Lindsay was proving she was a master at that. Before long the Sun was leading in the Eastern Conference. They went on to the WNBA finals that year, eventually losing to the Seattle Storm in a wrenching three-game series.

Lindsay did her part during the playoffs, where she nearly doubled her already impressive season average of 8.9 points to 15.4, led the team with a 4.6 assists, and made 28 of her 30 free throws. She was also selected to play in the historic WNBA vs. USA Basketball game at Radio City that season. Lindsay was hitting her stride as a pro.

She was meanwhile settling in to her new community. The people seemed to have the same Midwestern niceness she'd grown up with, and her growing throng of fans was just as polite. Lindsay, as is her nature, was just as polite to them in return.

"I remember one time after a hard fought game against the Monarchs in Sacramento," says Bill Tavares. "We'd won, and the team was being rushed off the floor to the locker room for post-game media interviews. As Lindsay passed by, a young boy called out for her autograph. It didn't seem apparent that she'd heard him, but from the hall she turned back to me and asked if I'd have the mother and son wait. True to her word, ten minutes later she appeared and gave him an autograph. That's her character, and I've witnessed it on numerous occasions. She's a better person than player, and she's a great player, so that's saying a lot."

Lindsay takes a free throw.

Along with her caring nature comes Lindsay's infamous penchant for practical jokes, and in those days Bill was often her target. On one occasion during a long flight to a game, the two discussed their passion for football and how badly they behaved when their team lost. Lindsay recalled that after the Atlanta Falcons upset her beloved Minnesota Vikings in the 1998-1999 NFC Championship game, she was so mad she kicked her dog down the stairs and blamed her sister. Bill was aghast. This was not the Lindsay he knew but her face was completely deadpan. Then it cracked with her contagious little smile. "Bill! I would never really do that!" She'd gotten him.

As avid as Lindsay was about her Vikings and Twins, it surprised her when she also began to feel a stake in the New England teams. "I can't help it," she says. "It's catchy. They're good, and their fans around here go crazy!"

By this time she was already beginning to realize that being drafted by an East Coast team had most probably been a good thing. Her skills were growing; she was fine tuning her game under circumstances that fully allowed it. It was a bit odd that in her ongoing play with the Sun, a team known for its striving, competitive ethos, she felt little stress or pressure. The only real pressure she had was self imposed, and nothing would ever eliminate that.

There's no way to know, she admits, what would have happened if she'd stayed in Minnesota, adding that it does no good to speculate. She just knew she was enjoying the chance Connecticut had given her, and could see the ways it was helping her mature both on and off the court. Dealing with the media was becoming easier, and the new surroundings were expanding her ability to adapt. Then there was the food.

"Can't get ones like that in Minnesota," she laughs, referring to New England lobsters.

She went back to Minnesota after the season to finish her degree, returning to Connecticut in January to help promote the 2005 season. The Sun franchise was chosen that year to host the sixth annual WNBA All-Star game on July ninth, a match-up between the Eastern and Western conferences that produced a total of 221 points and a first All-Star game dunk by Lisa Leslie. It was the most exciting game in WNBA All-Star history with more than nine thousand in attendance.

As in the previous year, Lindsay's play in 2005—her mix of flash handoffs and attentive reads of the minutest player action—helped the Sun to make the playoffs. The Sun knocked out Indiana in the finals for the Eastern Conference, but lost to the Sacramento Monarchs 3-1 in the WNBA finals, though they'd rather handily beaten them twice during the regular season with scores of 61-50 and 70-66. For Lindsay, the losses and two injuries she incurred during them were painful. She'd averaged 16.5 points in the semifinals before colliding with Indiana guard Tully Bevilaqua just seconds before the half-time buzzer during the second game. The damage appeared to be limited to soreness in her left knee, not enough to keep her from playing through the second half, but tests later showed she'd actually incurred a small fracture of the tibial plateau in her knee. It only kept her off the court a few days. She returned for game 1 of the finals, only to sprain her left ankle. She sat out game 2, but though she returned the next game, her play was not up to par. The Sun were ultimately defeated by Sacramento, who took the championship with a heart-stopping last-minute 3-pointer.

The ankle seemed to be healing properly at first, and Lindsay went to Europe during that off-season to play for Russia in the Euroleague. But it continued to bother her to the point of worry, and wasn't responding to rehabilitation. Surgery seemed to be the best solution.

"I'd sprained it so many times," she said, referring to injuries dating back to high school. "They told me those injuries had made my ligaments weaker and left scar tissue too, so it had to be fixed."

The surgery was performed in January, it was successful, and Lindsay was given a good chance for full recovery. She wore a cast for two weeks and did her best to baby it for the next four and a half months, following doctor's orders.

Lindsay knew the value of obeying orders. Her ankle was vital to her game. During that last season she'd averaged 12.1 points and 5.1 assist, and had a 27 point high in the semi-final game before getting hurt. It'd been a good streak up. All that mattered now was getting back in that shape.

For the rest of the off-season Lindsay served as an intern at the U of M as administrative assistant to her former Gopher coach, Pam Borton. There she did everything but coach and recruit (which would have been against NCAA rules), learning from the inside the workings of a team and gaining new perspectives. Her stint there also reunited her with her base comfort zone in H Town, as Hutchinson is familiarly known. Doing so never fails to recharge her.

She thoroughly enjoyed her time spent back home, but it didn't diminish her ever-increasing fondness of Connecticut. She'd made it her home away from home, and nearly became a part of Coach Thibault's family while recovering from her injury. She continued to enjoy the novelty of all things different but good around town—the seafood primarily. She liked the oyster bar in Mystic, a tourist area, but had an equal fondness for the steak restaurants right in the casino. The area beaches were great, and the proximity of Cape Cod with its beaches and New York with its sights and shopping led to mini-breaks that she thoroughly enjoyed.

By then she had also become quite comfortable exhibiting her wickedly dry sense of humor. One day, on a call to Bill Tavares to get a phone number she needed, she decided to first have some fun and faked being stranded, asking when in the world someone was going to pick her up after a grueling press conference. Bill panicked. He had no idea there'd been a press conference (and of course, there hadn't). As he proceeded to shout orders in the background in an attempt to fix such a horrible mess, Lindsay 'fessed up and politely requested the phone number she wanted.

Bill never did learn to see her zingers coming but he did catch on to her ways, which often left Lindsay's new teammate and friend Jessica Brungo to pick up the pieces. One time during a snowy road trip headed to a community relations event, Lindsay called Bill with fake news.

"Bill, the weather's terrible! Can't see a foot down the road! Don't know if we can ... oh no! A truck ... Look out!"

The silence sent shivers down Bill's back until Lindsay next spoke.

"Whew! We're okay, Bill. Almost got it from a Dole Raisin truck."

"A what?! Listen, turn around. Come back. I don't want you ..."

And then the background laughter.

When a real fender bender happened a few weeks later, Jess made the call. No way would Bill have believed Lindsay.

Either pulling teammates into her jokes or pulling a joke on them, Lindsay's deadpan delivery kept them on constant guard. Not that they minded. Her brand of humor, flying so calmly and straight out of the blue, alleviated the tension surrounding the seriousness of their jobs.

During the 2006 season the Sun seemed to be nearly unstoppable. All five of its starters—Lindsay, Katie Douglas,

Taj McWilliams-Franklin, Nykesha Sales, and Margo Dydek—were named to the WNBA All-Star team, a first in the WNBA history. Coach Mike Thibault was honored as the WNBA Coach of the Year. The playoffs went their way but the finals saw them lose to the Detroit Shock two games to one, a disappointing end to a most notable season.

When asked how it felt to play against her home state Lynx during those first years, Lindsay concedes to a range of emotions but adds that it's always about the win.

"It's not that hard to separate things. When you're on a team, it's all about the team," she states.

In Minnesota, it was different. The Lynx ran ads that their home girl Lindsay would be in town for a game. Her family and fans cheered for the Lynx and they cheered for her, too, fully understanding that was the way Lindsay would want it. For close family members like her Vilandre grandparents, who felt like celebrities themselves, those games became special events in a personal way.

"A group of preteen girls asked for my autograph once," said her grandmother with a proud smile. She was also often approached by churches and other groups organizing fund-raising events, and even by some elderly people who had followed Lindsay's career, all of whom knew the inside track a grandmother would have for autographs on pictures, T-shirts, or posters. She always did what she could to oblige.

Hopes were high back in Connecticut in 2007, after the team had come so close to the championship the year before, but a disappointing 5-10 start threatened to throw the team entirely off its game. The players rallied, winning 11 of the next 13 games, and eventually earned a spot in the playoffs. In the first round they faced the Indiana Fever, a team they'd beat in all four regular season games. They cruised through much of this game, too, but Indiana surged in the fourth quarter, forcing the first triple-overtime game in WNBA history. The Sun eventually took it by a five-point margin, but Indiana came back to win the next two. It was over. Connecticut was done. No conference finals this year.

A whirlwind off-season that year began with Lindsay and Ben's wedding, a quick three-day honeymoon, then she was off once again to play in the Euroleague, this time in Prague.

"At least this year Ben could come with me," She says. Participating in the Euroleague is something she's become accustomed to and does for several reasons. She loves the cultural experience, the learning involved in playing against new and different styles, and the physical consistency of staying in shape. It also provides an off-season income, a nice bonus well-used as she and Ben look to the future.

The Sun approached the 2008 season in an atmosphere of hopeful anxiety. The team had added several new players and lost a few, too. Gone was Katie Douglas, the face of the team, traded to Indiana for 6'2" Tamika Whitmore. Nykesha Sales would sit out the year with injuries, and center Margo Dydek was pregnant. Luck was not on their side. The virtually new team of starters required time to gel and get accustomed to one another, and pre-season predictions were that the Sun would not be contenders, at least not this year.

Boom. They opened the season with a phenomenal 8-1 record. Point guard Lindsay, now a seasoned veteran, was

Lindsay and Ben in the old town square in Prague.

using everything she knew, studying her new teammates' styles to lead effectively. Then, riding high, the team hit a five-game slump, something that had never happened before under Coach Thibault's watch. They managed to pull themselves together and finished the season at 21-13, good enough to place them second in the playoffs. At that point the new team fell to their inexperience. They were eliminated 1-2 in the first round by the New York Liberty.

For Lindsay herself it had been a good year, though she'd suffered a late-season ankle sprain. She was runner-up for the team MVP award, and was selected to the First Team All-WNBA for the first time in her career. In those New York playoff games, she'd led the league in assists per game with a 5.4 average, for which she was given the Peak Performance Award. In May and again in July, she was named the East's Player of the Week, and was noted as only the second player in WNBA history to average 10 points, 5 rebounds and 5 assists per game (Nikki Teasley having been the first to do so). Later that fall, Lindsay would go on to make the Euroleague All-Star team.

Honored as she was, Lindsay still felt the angst of the team's season end. They'd worked so hard, had done an exceptional job in making it as far as the playoffs, surprising even themselves. It just seemed such a shame to be stopped at that point.

Through it all she remained the same Lindsay, ever mindful of who she was and all that had contributed to her reaching this status. A fixture now in Connecticut and thankful for this second home, her hometown ties and her personable ways kept her in touch with her roots.

"She is a class act and a good friend," says John Mons, Operational Manager of Hutchinson's KDUZ radio station, who had become a family friend through his extensive coverage of Lindsay over the years. "She always takes the time to let you know just that. In September of 2008, my mother passed away and it was a difficult time. Even though Lindsay had more than enough on her mind with her professional basketball career, she took the time to contact me and let me know how sorry she was and that she was thinking of me. Needless to say, that meant more to me than words can ever say. Her unselfish gesture will never be forgotten. She hasn't changed a bit."

Fans in Connecticut had also come to recognize and appreciate Lindsay's unassuming ways and selfless abilities as a player, always giving away the ball when a teammate had better vantage. They were behind her and the team once again in 2009, eager to see how a year of play had brought the young team together as a competitive unit. Expectations were naturally high; this was the Connecticut Sun after all, they were champions if not a direct conference title holder. They would rebound and return to glory.

The season began with a string of losses, but they reversed the trend and won 7 of the next 10. Midway through the season they hosted the WNBA All-Star Game for the second time, a game that was nationally broadcasted by ABC. It was an honored beginning for the second half of the season, but further glory never materialized. A three-way tie for second place between the Sun, the Atlantic Dream, and the Washington Mystics going into the playoffs left them out cold. They finished the season in sixth overall place with a 16-18 record.

Lindsay had been forced to sit out through much of that trying time due to an eye injury she'd suffered in September. She'd been accidentally jabbed by an Indiana Fever player, resulting in a tear to her right iris. She would heal but could not participate in any games for a solid month, and was also forced to forego training camp for the USA Basketball Women's National Team.

As much as she regretted not being able to help her team, missing training camp was also a huge disappointment. She'd missed in 2007 because of her wedding, which made this time all the more regrettable. Still, she wasn't taking any chances.

"With some injuries, I just keep playing. But with this one, I won't risk my vision. I really want to be careful."

Doing as she was told, she healed and was ready to return to the Czech Republic to play again for Prague.

She'd been with Connecticut for six years by that fall,

and change was in the air. She was kept abreast of talks while in Europe and knew that as a free agent, she was in the mix. Coach Thibault had a lot to figure out before he'd be willing to let her go, but the opportunity for a shuffle was presenting itself and in all likelihood it would involve her. It was a decision Coach Thibault would have preferred not to make. Aside from all that Lindsay had contributed to the team, she had become almost a member of his family. But the overall interest of the team was paramount.

"I remember coming home one night to find Lindsay sitting with my son and his friends playing a board game. She fit right in, could trash talk right along with them. They were a good seven years younger but she didn't seem to notice. I think her home life with her brothers and sisters must have taught her how to adapt so well."

Lindsay's ability to laugh at herself and be the team's practical joker also made her presence important to team morale. She'd spend time in the coach's office going over questions or voicing opinions fearlessly, all in the name of learning and contributing to a team victory. She was as open to critique as she was praise. She'd spent the winter of her ankle recovery donating her time to community appearances, which created goodwill for the team and endeared her to the fans. They'd be disappointed to see her go.

With trade talks in the air, Lindsay remained agreeable and waited. Coach Thibault was well aware of her underlying desire to play for the Lynx. He didn't need to be reminded. Her job now was to concentrate on her play in Prague and let events take their course.

5

THE IMPACT OF INJURY

Injuries happen. They come with the territory, in basketball as in every sport, despite the efforts athletes take to remain in shape and safeguard their bodies. And while there is never an opportune time to have an injury, the timing of some injuries proves to be far more inconvenient, not to mention debilitating, than others.

Lindsay's injuries may be taken as a prime example.

Overall, she's been relatively accident free, given the length of her career and the seemingly carefree abandon of her play. Yet she's had her share of injuries, some more disrupting to the game than others, and some of lasting fitness concern. Lindsay takes them all as part of the game. She doesn't, however, take them lightly.

Sports injuries fall into two categories. The first is cumulative, occurring from overuse and tiring of a muscle, joint, or tendon. Such injuries usually just require time and rest to heal. The second, incurred during a traumatic incident, is acute. In basketball, the ankle and knee take the brunt of the action, and they're the two joints most commonly injured in both categories.

That's not to say a player can't hurt other body parts. In 2004, when Lindsay broke her right hand—her shooting hand—it was her first major injury and the timing could not have been worse. It occurred in February, at the peak of a Gophers hot streak and in the final months of Lindsay's four-year college career. She'd gone down following a collision and slammed her wrist to the floor, fracturing two metacarpal bones. Recovery meant four to six weeks on the bench. At the time, Lindsay was already the Gophers' all-time leading scorer and a serious contender for the Big Ten Player of the Year award. The team's streak had put them in prime position to advance deep into the NCAA tournament, perhaps all the way to the Final Four for a first time ever in the U of M's women's basketball history. It was a very inopportune time to lose a star player.

As devastating as the timing was for the team's prospects, it was also a setback to Lindsay's prospects of turning pro. She seemed to sense that as she was ushered off the floor, frantically searching the crowd to catch a familiar face. She caught her mother's eye and motioned her to follow. Lindsay desperately needed the kind of support that can only come from someone so close.

After the trainer had completed his examination, Lindsay and her mother sat alone in the locker room, waiting for the result. For the first time in her career, stretching back to her earliest days of rough and tumble hockey, she broke down in tears.

"Her motto always was that you don't cry over a game," Kathy says. "'It's only a game. It's only a sport. You don't cry over it. She always felt that way. That night was different, and I know, as her mother, it wasn't a cry over pain. She was definitely worried."

The day also happened to be Kathy's birthday. Lindsay hadn't wanted to spoil that for her, though celebrating was the farthest thing from her mother's mind at the moment.

The prognosis was a blend of good news and bad. Lindsay had broken two bones in her hand, and they would take four to six weeks to heal. There was a fair chance she'd heal sufficiently to continue playing. She obeyed orders and sat on the sidelines with her hand in a cast, cheering on the team as it finished the regular season with just five wins against seven losses. But the string of victories they'd amassed in their earlier hot streak still counted for something and they received a tenth-place ranking in the league going into the Big Ten Tournament.

During her time on the bench, Lindsay was receiving acupuncture treatments regularly (at her coach's recommendation) from specialist Dr. Metcalf, who'd helped other players with similar injuries. It worked. It worked beautifully. Lindsay credits the speed of her eventual full recovery in large part to those treatments. Kim (Nelson) Danlo also credits Lindsay's spunk and determination, which returned shortly after the initial shock of the injury. Lindsay was going to conquer.

"When Linds broke her hand toward the end of her senior season, you just knew that was not the way her career was going to end. The NCAA selection committee gave the Gophers a 7 seed ... and we all know how that turned out."

Yes, we do now. After five weeks of waiting it out, Lindsay returned near the end of March just in time to help the team take a first round win in the NCAA Tournament over the UCLA Bruins, scoring 31 points with her newly healed right hand. The crowd of over 12,000 went wild. The team went on to the semi-finals, where they lost to Connecticut, but the Gopher basketball women had gone farther than ever before toward a national championship.

Lindsay's return also coincided with an invitation from the Women's Basketball Coaches Association to play on the USA Senior National Team in the April 2004 WBCA All-Star Challenge. Despite her abbreviated season, Lindsay's statistics that year had put her among the elite performers in the nation.

All was well injury-wise until the next year, her first year in the pros, when Lindsay suffered the dreaded ankle and knee injuries, one happening right after the other. The knee injury occurred when she hyper-extended her left leg in a game against Indiana in the Eastern Conference finals. Bad timing again. Initial tests done at half-time showed no serious damage so she played the second half, scoring 13 of her team's 14 points in that half. Because of continued pain and swelling, however, an MRI was ordered the following day as a precaution, and it confirmed a small fracture of her tibial plateau in the anterior portion of her knee. Hope was high that she could continue playing, since the fracture was small and in an area that didn't receive much stress in motion.

For three days Lindsay underwent treatment averaging 12 hours a day, including both electrical stimulation and the acupuncture that had worked so well with her hand. Crutches helped the first day, she got by with a knee brace the second day, and by the third day the bruising was barely visible and the swelling had gone down to the point where her knee looked nearly normal. She practiced in the gym on the far end from the team, doing jump shots but taking care to avoid putting too much pressure on that leg, which was responding nicely. She soon got clearance to play if she felt it was right, since only she knew the feel of each pushing jump and turn.

When Lindsay woke up on the morning of the first game of the WNBA Finals, she knew she'd be able to help her team in the run for the title. The injury of just four days earlier had healed to the point where it was no longer of serious concern. She just knew. "I wasn't going to go out on the floor unless I knew I could perform 100 percent. If not, it wouldn't do my leg or the team any good."

The game was against the Western Conference champions, the Sacramento Monarchs, the first in a best-of-five series. It was the Sun's second appearance in the finals, the Monarchs' first. Lindsay was ready to do her part and was thrilled that her leg was cooperating. She played 25 minutes with no turnovers, although she knew she was holding back ever so slightly, nursing her damaged leg. Her shooting wasn't up to par but it would come back as the game progressed. It wasn't a game to hold back in, or have anything go wrong. Then it did. A twist of her left ankle in a play that happened too fast to seem out of the ordinary brought a cringe to her face. She was whisked to the locker room. She was out for the game.

Lindsay knew what an ankle sprain could do. She'd had

one in high school. In light of that, she'd begun a career-long habit in college, at her trainer's insistence, of having both ankles taped before every game. It was a good precaution and undoubtedly prevented some unwanted damage. She'd been taped for this game too, but the taping couldn't prevent this particular bend.

She sat out game two, helplessly watching her team lose to the Monarchs. After being iced and bandaged, Lindsay was back on the floor for game three. She struggled, knowing she wasn't playing at her best, and managed only 2 points and 2 assists with 5 turnovers in the first 23 minutes she played. In game four, Lindsay was in for 26 minutes and had 3 points, 6 rebounds, and 5 assists, but 4 turnovers. The Monarchs won that day, taking the championship 3 to 1. Lindsay admits the injury had taken its toll.

"Going into that game, my goal was to put the injury out of my mind and give the team all I had. I feel that's what I did. It was all I could do."

While there's no way to know how the season would have ended if Lindsay hadn't been injured, it was perhaps the most unfortunate and untimely one of her career. It also led to surgery a few months later. Her ankle wasn't responding to rehabilitation the way it should have, and surgery was deemed necessary to repair it properly, especially considering the promising professional career that lay ahead of her. Scar tissue from her previous sprain in high school was removed, and the surrounding ligaments were reconstructed. The operation was performed in Connecticut, far from home, but Coach Thibault's family became hers for a good deal of the time. It was a lovely gesture that pleased his wife and kids as much as Lindsay. She was in a cast for two weeks, then faced four and a half months of rehabilitation. She returned to the court in May just in time for Connecticut's next season.

Just before rehab Lindsay had a brief and rare respite which she spent traveling with Ben on his Canadian Tour, which had rounds at that time in Arizona and Texas. She came out to watch him play every day, though she hobbled around in a walking boot and stayed pretty close to the clubhouse. She was just happy to be with him and he was thrilled to have her there. Sometimes injuries do have silver linings.

With her left ankle fully healed, in 2008 Lindsay proceeded to sprain her right one. Both are healthy now—although she can't wear high heels—and she continues to wear tape for protection against further injury. "I've gotten so used to the tape I'd really feel bare without it." Her trainers still insist on it anyway, leaving her no choice in the matter.

With no more ankles left to sprain (knock on wood) it was on to a broken nose. The mishap occurred as she was driving to the hoop for a lay-up. That injury merely required wearing a mask that reminded her of her old hockey days. Lindsay took that one like a pro and waited out the healing, simply looking rather strange and scaring little children.

She wasn't so fortunate the next time. A misplaced opponent's elbow resulted in a torn iris in Lindsay's eye. In this case, the concern for lost playing time took a back seat to a greater concern for the injured eye itself. "You don't mess around with your vision," she said, fully knowing that not following doctor's orders to safeguard it could have resulted in permanent vision loss. Those orders were to have no physical activity that might jostle the eye for at least a month.

While she's always adhered to doctors' orders, in this instance Lindsay felt it of special importance and carefully avoided any and all unnecessary activity. "Sometimes I've played right through an injury when I know it's just a matter of being able to do it and not make anything worse. All athletes do that. This was different." So she took it easy, giving up training camp for the USA Basketball Women's National Team, which she'd been elected to shortly before the injury. It was disappointing to miss the camp, but necessary. She attended the training in Washington DC for the six days of play, watching the best she could, and was very pleased to hear later she was in the running for the national team's Olympic selection. Coupled with the good news that her vision would be fully restored, life was looking good.

Injuries count for the majority of time a player is out of commission, since everyday illnesses usually don't stop a player from performing. Lindsay herself can only remember missing three games in her whole career due to illness, and those involved strep throat and high fevers. Players who spend the winter season in the Euroleague seem to contract colds more frequently than they do in the summer WNBA games, but such things don't normally keep a player off the court.

Yet debilitating injuries happen less frequently than might be expected, considering the high energy levels involved and the very nature of competitive play. When it comes to being the cause of an injury to another, Lindsay says, "No one ever intends to do it. It's just a physical game and those things happen. It's not anyone's fault." She also observes how an injury to one player can make the others step up their games. "It forces them to improvise which improves their plays."

That was the case in 2004 when Lindsay broke her hand. Everyone put in their all, and Janel McCarville, seeming to double her already show-stopping efforts, scored 23 points, 11 rebounds, and 10 steals against Ohio State after Lindsay was out of play. It was a first ever triple-double in Big Ten Tournament history. Though the team incurred numerous loses during Lindsay's absence, it definitely wasn't due to any lack of trying.

Lindsay would occasionally take the sting out of a teammate's minor injury by using her infamous humor. Once, when Janel took a hit and landed flatly on the floor, Lindsay reassured the ref, saying, "She's okay, don't worry about her. She had worse things happen to her in that Mexican prison." It was a fib, of course, part of an inside and running joke the whole team shared. It lightened the moment, rallied team spirit, and briefly took Janel's thoughts off her pain.

If there's a redeeming quality to injuries, minor or severe, it can be seen in the way it pulls a team together, forcing others to step up to the plate and underscoring the players' concern for one another. Of all the possible silver linings that can arise from the ruins, it is those that make the aftermath a bit easier to take and show the game to be exactly what it is, a team effort, injuries included.

Would Lindsay ever let the possibility of further injury stop her from continuing to play? Not in a million years.

6

BEN

Lindsay and Ben Greve's wedding on October 6, 2007, was a beautiful beginning to a new life and marked the end of a courtship that had taken Ben from state to state and even to Europe in order to spend time with her. His schedule was nearly as demanding as hers, but he managed as much time as he could, never seeming to mind the inconveniences it often included. Lindsay was most thankful for that.

Although they'd grown up within fifty miles of each other, the two didn't meet until a college statistics class during Lindsay's sophomore year in college. (They're the same age, but Ben had missed a full year due to illness, and graduated one year behind her.) "I thought she was really cute so I started showing up a little earlier for class trying to sit by her. As I got to know her, I summoned up the courage to ask her out. She said yes. Our first date was dinner and a movie."

On that first date Ben learned there was a very funny girl behind the cute face. "As I got to know her, I couldn't help but love her personality. She has a great sense of humor, she's really quick, and has a good dry wit." It was enough for him to want to learn more, and Lindsay felt the same way about Ben, though their often-conflicting schedules made for years of a drawn out relationship before those wedding bells could ring.

While most couples spend months deciding on the details of their upcoming big day, in Lindsay and Ben's situation many of the tasks fell to their mothers. Ben's golf-tour schedule allowed him time to pitch in more than Lindsay, who was in Connecticut in the midst of regular season push with a playoff berth still within reach. The mothers didn't mind, they'd become good friends, and Lindsay trusted them completely to know what she and Ben had in mind. She helped as often as she could long distance, and loved having her mom come for a week to join in finding just the right bridal gown and bridesmaids' dresses. Despite the obstacles of time and distance, along with the dilemma of not knowing exactly when the wedding would be, the planning worked well and was actually fun for everyone involved.

Lindsay had become like a daughter to Ben's parents from the earliest days of their relationship, when Lindsay Whalen wasn't yet a household name. The person they found so charming and personable impressed them on her own merit. At the time she and Ben were just two kids who obviously had something special between them.

"We instantly liked her," says Sandy Greve. "She fit right into our family. She got my jokes, she was comfortable, she could be one of the boys when it came to sports but was always still very much a sweet girl."

Dave and Sandy Greve both teach in the school district of Annandale, a city located just north of Hutchinson. Ben is the oldest of three sons. Like the Whalens, the Greve's are a very close-knit family with sports playing a big part in their activities together. The boys have all played football, basketball, or golf in either high school or college. Tim, the youngest, was a member of the Annandale Cardinal basketball team the year they went to the state tournament, and continued his love of basketball with an internship as athletic trainer for the Minnesota Timberwolves. He's currently enrolled in graduate school at Concordia in St. Paul.

Tragically, Ben's brother Nick, 26, in the summer of 2010. He was an amazing young man, a dedicated son, brother, and friend, and losing him has been a devastation to this extremely close family and all who knew him. He, too, had always been an avid sportsman with a passion for golf. He graduated from Gustavus Adolphus College in 2007 with a degree in accounting and was employed in Eden Prairie as an auditor for the firm of Boulay, Heutmaker & Zibell. His trademark smile will always remain in the hearts and memories of those fortunate enough to have known him.

When Lindsay first came into Ben's life, both Nick and Tim adopted her as the sister they never had, and a dream one at that. She had no trouble taking them on in a backyard game of touch football or on the front driveway for hoops. While she's no slouch at football, having had lots of practice with her siblings growing up, in hoops she was a force to be reckoned with, moving and shooting so quickly that even they, proficient as they were themselves, were amazed.

Lindsay and Ben with the pink roadster she rode in as a Grand Marshall at the U of M homecoming in 2009.

When it came to board games or cards, their favorite indoor activities, she was again a worthy opponent. Any game with a challenge suited all of them, especially this new sister.

All three Greve siblings were avid golfers but Ben has taken it to a career level. He lettered from 7th grade on in golf and won the state high school individual title in his junior year at Annandale High, where he was also a member of the National Honor Society. He was all-conference three of his high school years in basketball and one year in football, but golf was his paramount sport. Recognizing his passion and talent, his parents have always been supportive of his ambitious path.

Ben was recruited for golf by the U of M and was on the team in 2002 when they took both the Big Ten Championship and the National Championship. In 2003, after winning the NCAA Championship, the team took a trip to the White House and met with President Bush. Ben was named to the All-Big Ten Team in 2004 and in 2005 was team captain and MVP. He also individually won the Michigan State Bruce Fossum Invitational in 2005, as well as a Big Ten Men's Golfer of the Week award.

After graduating in business and advertising, Ben began his professional career with a year on the National Golf Association Hooters Tour, followed by a year with the Dakotas Tour. He was on the brink of rejoining the Hooters Tour, which would have kept him mainly on the East Coast near Lindsay, when he learned he'd qualified for the more prestigious Canadian Tour. He has not yet qualified for the PGA tour, though in an attempt he missed by a single stroke in the second round (of three) in that extremely competitive competition.

One of the many things Dave and Sandy Greve saw early on and admired in Lindsay was her support of Ben in his career. Ben in turn feels the same about Lindsay's. That's often not easy in a two-career relationship, especially when their paths take them in wildly different directions. Before

Above: after the wedding. Below: Lindsay and her bridesmaids.

they were married, Ben lived with relatives and friends close to his tour areas, coming home as often as possible, though seeing Lindsay there was a matter of hit-and-miss since her schedule varied as much as his. Their longest stretch of separation was during her first year overseas in Russia, when they were apart for three months, although he was able to join her for two months later. Her stateside play made life easier, with Ben doing a two- to three-week sprint on a tour, then having a week off to spend with her. They did what they could to make it work.

News of their engagement in May of 2007 reached the Connecticut newspaper the day after it happened and made its way to Minnesota just as quickly. Getting engaged was the easy part; setting a date for an wedding was something else. With neither of their schedules set in stone due to the variables of playoffs and championships, a tentative date had to do until a firm date could be set, invitations sent out, and reservations finalized for a church and reception hall.

Finally everything came together. The date was set: October 6th. St. Anastasia Catholic Church in Hutchinson, Lindsay's home parish, was reserved, and former neighbor Sean David Moses McGraw, now a Holy Cross priest, was flown by Lindsay and Ben from Ireland to perform the ceremony.

The day was beautiful and the service special in the lovely, familiar church. All of Lindsay's and Ben's siblings were in the wedding party, along with a number of their friends. Lindsay's youngest brother, comical Thomas, proudly served as the self-titled head usher. The reception was held at the

Hutchinson Event Center, large enough to hold the more-than-three-hundred guests. Coach Thibault and his family came from Connecticut; Coach Borton, among others, came from the U of M. Teammates from Lindsay's various teams and Ben's golfing colleagues combined with friends from childhood, high school and college came to celebrate. It was a perfect send-off to their new life ahead.

The reality of scheduling struck once again soon after the big day. Lindsay was due in Prague for her first season there playing for the Euroleague during her WNBA break. After a very brief honeymoon in Wisconsin, she hopped a fifteen-hour flight overseas. Ben had a tour commitment to fulfill and couldn't go with her. It was two long, lonely weeks for both of them. Being apart when dating was one thing—being married gave it a completely different feeling. For Lindsay, it was the loneliest two weeks of her life.

Ben had the advantage of being on familiar ground but otherwise was not faring any better. He finished his tour obligations and headed to the apartment she'd arranged for them in Prague. Within a short time they began adjusting, glad to be with each other again and excited to begin learning the ins and outs of Prague, from discovering favorite restaurants to the latest movies, both of them being food and movie buffs. They had not yet devised a sophisticated means of communicating with family back home, so were pretty much on their own that first year. They settled into married life on the other side of the world from all they knew. It was alright. They were in love.

They now look at Prague as their home away from home,

and their schedules, although at times still a juggling act, have quieted into more of a pattern. Ben worked as a club pro in Connecticut at the Black Hall Club while Lindsay was in her regular season there, then was able to live in Prague for the winter season since his Canadian Tour didn't conflict. He adapted to both places well, finding a great practice spot in Connecticut to keep up his game while getting to know the area.

When Lindsay was playing in Connecticut he'd be right at the games, sitting quietly but intently. He quickly became friends with the other players' husbands and together they watched their wives from a prized section of the bleachers. He isn't the type to overtly protest a perceived bad call by a ref, it's just not who he is, but like Lindsay, he's perfectly accepting of those who do. "I loved watching games with V," he says of Vasilis Giapalakis, the Sun's Katie Douglas's husband. "He's good entertainment. Watching him get worked up was always part of a good game."

Ben now works as a club professional with the Medina Golf and Country Club in Minnesota, and also plays the Dakota Tour. The juggling of schedules is less hectic now than it used to be, though the travel that both his and Lindsay's careers require will be a part of their lives for a good while to come. They take it in stride as they do everything, both sharing low-key personalities and a philosophy of live-and-let-live. The lifestyle suites them, and they perfectly suit each other.

Top: Lindsay Lieser, Kim Danlo, Lindsay, and Angel Leon goofing around.
Botom: Ben and Lindsay dining out with friends in Prague.

7

OFF COURT

The side of Lindsay we see on the court—the aggressive go-getter with a competitive edge so sharp it could be steel—differs from the off-court Lindsay in some, but not all, respects. Off court she displays more of her mild temperament and easy-going homebody ways, though sparks of her competitive spirit remain pronounced. In fact, competition is involved in nearly everything Lindsay does, whether it be against an opponent on the floor or in a contest of video game skills. The aggressiveness she shows on court, however, rarely appears even mildly off court, although it will when someone is late.

"Lindsay has one pet peeve, and that's when people aren't on time," her mother Kathy reports. "To her, if you're ten minutes early, you're late. She applies it to herself too, but that rarely happens. She's the most punctual person I know."

The punctuality Lindsay values can't really be attributed to her career in basketball since it started long before her feet ever hit a court. It's just a part of who she is. But considering the demanding schedule she keeps now, with games, practices, and service commitments on top of her personal and family life, it's understandable why it's grown.

Her actual off-court time isn't what it may seem to those not living the life. Players generally have the day following a game off, otherwise all days have practice. The breaks between seasons, at least for those who, like Lindsay, play overseas, vary from a few days to as much as a month, depending on how late regular season playoffs run. Regardless, the time away from the court is necessarily spent by Lindsay and others in relaxing and having a normal life.

Normal for Lindsay involves video games—she's been addicted to them for as long as they've been around—and movies. Her favorites range from *The Fugitive* with Tommy Lee Jones to Ben Affleck's *Pearl Harbor*, and of course *Hoosiers* with Gene Hackman. In Prague, she and Ben often found movies in English which allowed them to keep up with current releases. When she was younger it was *Duck Tails*; she loved the idea of swimming in money like Uncle Scrooge, says her father Neil. When she likes a movie she tends to watch it over and over and liberally interjects lines from her favorites into normal conversation just to kick up things for fun.

When time allows, she and Ben like taking road trips, more often than not with a work-related angle involved. Besides the sheer adventure, it's the time spent together away from daily obligations that makes for relaxing mini-vacations, which is all they can usually squeeze in between their many commitments. Their combined stateside and overseas travels have allowed them to see a great deal of the world, and they soak up the local atmosphere and history wherever they go, especially in

Europe, where there seems to be no end to new experiences.

Lindsay's away games, plus her overseas play in the Euroleague during the winter season, have also given her parents and often the whole family a chance to explore new places. "We feel very fortunate to have done so many things together," says her mom, Kathy. "We wouldn't have had the chance if it wasn't for the travel we did for her games and to visit her in Europe. It's been a very blessed life for all of us."

The traveling for Lindsay, especially the road trips, also means eating in restaurants, which ranks high on the list of fun things to do along with video games and movies. Lindsay has loved to eat out since childhood and has always been anxious to try a new place or a new item at an old standby, and almost always goes for appetizers and desserts. As a kid, in addition to family visits to Valley Fair Amusement Park, she and her dad made an annual event of hitting the Minnesota State Fair together in the opening days of its run, primarily to sample all the food stands, a ritual they mutually relished. Considering the amount of energy she's always burned, this love of fueling up is logical.

It should come as no surprise that restaurants are now a big part of Lindsay's life with Ben. She still has an eye for something new and Ben is always game as well, though they're often hungry for the tried-and-true menus of their routine hangouts. In a twist of fate, Ben is allergic to seafood, one of Lindsay's all-time favorites, but he's not so allergic that he can't watch her down a few shrimp while enjoying his own plate of steak. It's never been a big problem.

They have a large number of friends, most of them gathered

over the years through contact with others in their fields. For Lindsay, her teammates from the ever-changing teams at the U of M and Connecticut are still a part of her life, friends like Lindsay Lieser, Kim Danlo, Emily Inglis and Jess Brungo, who were all attendants at her wedding along with her sisters. Many of the husbands, like another dear teammate Katie Douglas's, have become couples friends with Lindsay and Ben, and it works that way too with the friends Ben brought into the relationship. They never have a shortage of things to do or chums on hand to share in the fun.

When she's able, Lindsay also joins her group from high school, who still get together in the longest of most wonderful friendships. They take an annual February weekend trip skiing or whatever sounds good that year; they throw each other bachelor parties, attend weddings, are there for each other at births, deaths, and events in between. Lindsay has missed many of those events only because of her schedule, but remains as much a part of the group as ever. Some go as far back as grade school in the group that includes—now most with married names—Emily Inglis, Katie Bruestle, Emily Reiter, Erika Uldbjerg, Naomi Brown, Mackenzie Schlect, Anne Brugman, Kristin Pulkrabek, Courtney Thode, Sarah Huiskes, Katie Pearce, Kelli Fernholtz, and Lindsay. A group of thirteen for jersey #13—a very cool coincidence.

When not with friends, eating, or lounging as comfy homebodies, Lindsay and Ben like to golf together, although the chance only arises a few times a year. Lindsay dabbled in golf long before she met Ben, and although she fully acknowledges he's the family champ, she manages to keep up alongside him. Much of her experience came from playing with her dad. Says Ben, "She is very competitive on the course, especially when she's playing with her dad. Neither one likes to lose to the other, so it's pretty entertaining to watch."

Her grandfather Vilandre attests to her determination. He set her up with a golf lesson when she was young and came back to find a wide-eyed instructor very impressed with her game. She later participated in a few charity golf tournaments at the Bemidji Country Club as a favor to him, and proved to be so good he was jokingly accused of "loading" his team with a pro. Whatever Lindsay does, especially when it comes to athletics, she strives to do well, using a mix of raw athletic talent and pure grit.

Grandpa and Grandma are affectionately known to her as "Gpa" and "Gma" in her habit of nicknaming everyone close. Aunts and uncles get a similar label with shortcuts like "UB" for Uncle Brian. It's all part of her sense of humor, and a way of letting them know she cares. She's given Ben several nicknames over the years, and he's come up with a few for her, too, all within the couple's vein of humor.

As much as they care for their friends, Ben and Lindsay also spent a great deal of time with their families, and both are very close to the other's. They simply enjoy their company. Lindsay has had a special relationship with both her parents at different times in her life. When younger, she and her dad bonded over sports at a time when her mother was busy with the younger children. When they weren't on the rink or in the yard shooting hoops, the two were hunched over the kitchen table, with Neil reading the sports page aloud to Lindsay, hashing over Sid Hartman's column or the latest Vikings, Northstars, or Gopher scores. From kindergarten on, he would take her to at least one day of every state hockey tournament. With that, plus coaching her in actual hockey, they had an enviable father-daughter relationship. When she was in high school they developed a pre-game routine of Neil making a meal of noodles and sauce (a favorite she's grown tired of by now) and after the game it was off for a Whopper. Lindsay still calls him after every game—a nice, longstanding ritual. They still share that special closeness, talking often by phone when unable to visit in person. It was a foundation deeply rooted in love and common interest, and remains special in its own right.

Meanwhile, as times changed, Lindsay and her mother found their own special bond. It had always been there, it just became newer with each passing year as Lindsay grew in areas other than sports. The two talk every day now, by phone or in person, and Lindsay depends on Kathy whether she's happy or down or just needs an ear. They've also had some great times together, mother and daughter, often with a sister or two included.

"In Lindsay's first year being a pro in CT, my daughter Katie and I went out for Memorial Day weekend, and on one of the days we decided to check out a beach near where she was living. It was sunny but cold; still we were determined to sit on the beach on Long Island Sound. Lindsay earlier that year had received a promise ring from Ben, and she took it off when we got to the beach so she wouldn't lose it or get it full of sand. She neglected to tell Katie and I that she had

Lindsay and her mom Kathy.

put it in a plastic Walmart bag we had with us, so Katie and I proceeded to use the bag for garbage.

"So we sit in the sun, and at the end of our day we're getting ready to head back to her apartment when Lindsay started looking for her ring, telling us where she'd put it. But the bag had been tossed around so much throughout the day the ring was no longer in it. After much searching and presumed unanswered prayers, Lindsay and I drive to Home Depot, leaving Katie in the wind and cold so we wouldn't forget where we were sitting, to buy a metal detector. We went back and used it but still no luck.

"After hours of searching, we decided to give up. In the beginning, Lindsay said, 'If we find the ring, I'm jumping into the Atlantic.' It's freezing cold water. Just as we were getting ready to go, we picked up one of our chairs and underneath it, I notice something shiny. Sure enough, there was her ring! We were so ecstatic both Lindsay and Katie ran into the Atlantic!"

There have been fun times, indeed, amidst a hectic life.

Still, wherever she goes and whatever she does, Lindsay's job and who she is never is far from sight. Mixed into the freedom of her time off are autograph signings and community relations events for the team. She does them all gladly, doing anything to support her sport and to encourage young girls to follow their ideals. Some activities are strictly for fun or for the novelty of the experience, like doing a game analysis for ESPN and throwing out the ceremonial ball for the Twins. Others have a more pointed goal.

She speaks at basketball camps, the most recent being Coach Pam Borton's "Be a Champ Camp" for aspiring young basketball players. With some of the girls in #13 jerseys and their parents present as well, Lindsay addressed the handling of school and sports, answered all the girls' questions, and gave pointers in actual drills before signing autographs for the grateful group. She considers doing such things an honor.

There are charity events, team-sponsored interviews, and public appearances. Honored as she feels to do them all, there are some events specifically designed to directly honor her in return. She's humbled to accept.

"Linds has been noted on many occasions for her modesty and calm demeanor on the court," says childhood friend Emily. "To those who see her in her daily life, this is evident off the court as well. I remember her calling me around the time we graduated from college, and she wanted me to

Lindsay signing autographs.

help her get ready for a photo shoot. She came over, and we did her hair and picked out an outfit. When I asked her what it was for, she again told me it was 'just a photo shoot.' The next day, I saw her on the front page as the athlete of the year. A friend since kindergarten, and she still had to be directly asked if she was being photographed for something in particular."

Those kinds of honors are no small recognitions. Lindsay was also chosen as one of six grand marshals for the U of M's homecoming parade in 2009. The other five:

Walter Mondale, former vice president of the United States and world leader in his service as ambassador to Japan. He also served as a United States senator.

Bobby Bell, NFL hall of Famer. As a linebacker, he took the Kansas City Chiefs to Super Bowl victory in 1970, and was a two-time All-American Gopher football star who led the Gophers to a Rose Bowl victory and a national championship.

Norman Borlaug, recipient of the Nobel Peace Prize, also the Congressional Gold Medal and the Presidential Medal of Freedom. He's known as the Father of the Green Revolution.

Deb Hopp, vice president of publishing for MSP communications which publishes the *Minneapolis-St. Paul Magazine*. Deb is an influential area leader and past head of the United Way campaign.

Garrison Keillor, author, humorist, creator of A Prairie Home Companion radio show and co-writer and star of the same titled movie. He has been published in *The Atlantic Monthly*, *Time*, and the *New Yorker*.

The six, representing more than 400,000 living U of M graduates who have gone on to do their part in creating a better world, were chosen for their achievements and leadership. It's difficult to be humble in such company, but Lindsay, while fully acknowledging her success and taking great pride in all she's done, remains the person who sees herself as simply doing what she's been put here to do.

In 2010 she was again acknowledged by being chosen as grand marshal of the Aquatennial Celebration in Minneapolis. Lindsay loved every minute of it, and has grown to like this part of her life nearly as much as playing. Almost ... but not quite. Her heart will forever be in the game.

8

It's Game Day

A ll athletes have a way of approaching a big event. Before they ever touch the floor, track, field, or water, they've gone through a routine to prepare, both physically and psychologically. Lindsay's routine, while similar to that of many other basketball players, has its own system, complete with vital personal touches.

Routines are important for several reasons. They raise an athlete's comfort level in the hours preceding an important competition, when anxiety tends to be high. Comfort leads to confidence and a sense of being in "sync," which can spell the difference between having a good game and feeling "off." Routines also take the effort out of deciding what to eat, when to leave, which allows a player to focus on the more important matter of the upcoming game.

Finally, observing a routine adds to an athlete's sense of control, which can be extended to the court or field where the challenges are far greater. And many athletes, including Lindsay, keep elements of their game-day routine on practice days and even during the off-season. Eating the same, sleeping and exercising the same helps maintain the momentum so the body and mind are ready when game day arrives once more.

LINDSAY'S GAME DAY ROUTINE

The day before a game can be as important as the game day itself. On those days it's Lindsay's habit not to do anything very strenuous other than practice in the morning, then nap if at all possible and have a decent meal for dinner. Often that meal is a high carbohydrate feast including some sort of pasta with salads, though in recent years she's begun to mix things up by more often eating rice and fish or chicken. She actually prefers to go out for that meal, and considers dining out at any time as "one of life's pleasures." On the night before a game day, eating out also saves her having to cook or clean up the kitchen. After dinner she relaxes with a movie or light entertainment and tries to be in bed by 10:00.

On a day when a home game has been scheduled with a normal start time of 7 p.m. Lindsay's routine looks like this:

7:30

She wakes with coffee and something simple, not hungry yet but needing a bit of nourishment—anything from cold cereal to toast, depending on what's on hand and what sounds good at the moment.

8:45

Lindsay arrives at the gym for treatment with her trainer, including an ultrasound on her Achilles tendon, before starting warm-ups.

9:30

The team and coaches go over play tapes of the opposing team for that night's game.

10:00

Time for shoot around with the team.

11:00

The team has a brief practice session that concentrates on anticipated plays for the upcoming game.

11:45

Home to eat a substantial brunch. Lindsay estimates hers remains the same roughly 80 percent of the time: three slices of turkey bacon, eggs, Eggo waffles, fruit—usually a banana—and yogurt. She will sometimes vary it slightly or substitute a hearty sandwich, but prefers to stick to her regulars.

1:00

It's time for a power nap as the afternoon gets to be long and resting is vital to sustain energy throughout the upcoming evening. It's never a time for shopping or errands. She isn't always able to fall into a deep sleep, but watching a little television helps slow her down and contributes to the idea of rest. When she does watch, she'll turn the set off for the last hour, shut her eyes, and fall into the deepest sleep that will come.

4:00

Upon waking she recharges with a light snack, seldom varying a routine that involves peanut butter and jelly on toast along with a cup of coffee.

4:30

Back to the locker room for pre-game treatment, the icing and taping of her ankles.

5:00

It's time for stretching, warm-ups and practice shoots on the court.

6:40

The team clears the floor and heads to the locker room for a pep talk 20 minutes before game start time.

AFTER THE GAME

When the autographs have been signed and showers taken, the players are done work for the day and most are extremely hungry. Lindsay likes to go out for that late meal, either with Ben, with family if they've attended the game, or with teammates. Then it's off to sleep with the anticipation of having the following day to do as she chooses, since it's customarily the one day of no practice.

Away games are different only in that the team often flies in and out at irregular times and game times tend to vary. Otherwise, the hotel stays and local gyms offer the same opportunity Lindsay has at home to stick to the routines described above, and the trainers who accompany the team know all the familiar drills and treatments.

Routines depend no only on circumstances but on particular team structure as well. In Connecticut, food and sleep were of her choosing, but warm-ups were conducted separately rather than as a team. The differences require mindset alterations but come rather quickly once a season begins.

The distinction between routine and superstition is subtle but definite. Routines don't usually vary much after a win or a loss, and serve the purpose of alleviating a player's unnecessary stress. Superstitions usually change based on the results they produce, and, when skipped or not performed correctly, can actually add to a player's stress rather than alleviate it.

Yet superstitions are such an integral part of playing for so many athletes, they've been accepted and are even considered normal. Many are rooted in the belief that a seemingly arbitrary action or object—touching a specific railing or wearing a special pair of socks night after night— has the power to determine performance. The lack of a logical connection between the action and the outcome isn't relevant. Most are quite harmless, and few athletes consider them a substitute for hard work or training, but in some cases they may begin to resemble obsessive-compulsive behavior. Most develop by chance and continue to be observed only so long as they work. Chewing a certain flavor of gum during the course of a winning game might initiate a habit, but chewing that same "lucky" flavor in a loss will make it suddenly useless. Superstitions are picked up and dropped as needed, while routines often have little variance. Superstitions are mental tricks and players know it, but that doesn't decrease their magic.

Lindsay's superstitions have varied over the years, some dropped and others altered or added. There's one that has stayed true in its form and will always remain because it's carried over from her dad. Nobody is allowed to get a haircut on game day. She's not shy about letting everyone know. If she had her way, no player, no coach, and not a single fan in the stands would get a haircut on the day of a game.

"No haircut on game day. Ever. It's just one of those things that matter, I suppose because of my dad. If it worked for him, I'm not messing with it."

Lindsay has only one other stringent superstition: she always says an Our Father and a Hail Mary during the National Anthem. "I don't pray for a win or anything like that, God has bigger things to worry about. I just pray that no one gets injured playing, and that everybody, my family if they're coming, has made it safely to the game."

When it comes to injuries, she knocks on wood at the mention of hers or anyone else's, or when conversation turns to the possibility of one even happening. She has a feeling it helps.

Lindsay always shakes the hand of her trainer before being taped or iced, with the handshake taking on various configurations. After a win, that handshake stays the same until a loss when it becomes something new. And she insists on having her ankles taped in the proper order—left first, then the right. It's just one of those things.

A ritual she had with chewing gum has grown less rigid over the years. She likes to pop a piece right before a game for good breath and a refreshing little jolt, but refuses to step onto the court floor with it still in her mouth. The habit of removing her gum before touching the court may have started as a way to insure that she wouldn't start the actual game chewing it, which would have driven her crazy. She still chews it fairly often and dumps it at the entrance, but isn't quite as concerned about her foot accidentally touching the court as she used to be. Seems it didn't affect the game outcome.

Some superstitions develop by accident. For example, her grandpa and grandma Vilandre once wore t-shirts to a game with lettering announcing they were Lindsay Whalen's grandparents emblazoned on the front. It was the Big Ten tournament game in Indianapolis and friends had surprised them with the shirts as gifts in celebration. Unfortunately, Lindsay's U of M team lost that game, so Lindsay politely suggested in no uncertain terms that those shirts should stay in the closet forever.

She has a habit that isn't likely to change of wiping her hands on the foot Slip Not board before each game. "I realize it's filthy dirty but so is the ball so I guess it doesn't matter." It gives her a better grip of the ball, which makes it very practical, but needing the feel of it every game now qualifies it as having a touch of superstition.

When all is said and done, and the game has been won or lost, Lindsay's attitude is to carry on doing the best she can and use whatever helps her to do that. Other than to take from each game what worked or didn't, including the incidentals that may or may not matter, there isn't anything that can be done to change an outcome. She always approaches each game day with high expectations, then faces the results with the same view she has toward life. "If you take it too seriously, especially a loss, it can really affect the next game. A win is a win, a loss is a loss. That's the only way I can look at it."

Lindsay being interviewed after a game in Prague.

9

OFF TO EUROPE

The fall of 2010 will see Lindsay making her fifth regular off-season trip to play for the Euroleague, Europe's highest level professional basketball competition. The league is comprised of teams from more than twenty countries, divided into groups for a round-robin style of play followed by knock-out rounds leading to a Final Four. Teams are admitted based on a variety of criteria, including their performance in domestic leagues, home attendance, and the result of the previous year's Euroleague event. The games are broadcast in 191 countries including the United States.

Following a year with the Russian team in Ekaterinburg, Lindsay has played all subsequent years for ZVVZ USK Prague in the Czech Republic. She is one of roughly a hundred players from the WNBA who play in the Euroleague during the off season. The opportunity to play point guard overseas has helped advance her skills by exposing her to a variety of new and effective moves learned from players trained in different traditions. The cultural exchange on and off the court has broadened Lindsay as both a player and person.

Participating on a Euroleague team has several advantages for WNBA players, from the study of play to the flexibility and knowledge gained by adjusting to international rules. There is also significant money involved. While the WNBA operates within a capped salary structure, the Euroleague does not, and the difference can be substantial. Perks such as cars and rent-free living arrangements are often added for players' convenience as well. During Lindsay's first season she received a car and shared a complimentary apartment with a Russian teammate, then in Prague had her own apartment, which by then she was sharing with Ben.

The benefits aside, those WNBA players who also play in the Euroleague work virtually all year round. Add in the travel and relocating involved, and the schedule can be rather exhausting. Some players eventually abandon one or the other league, often opting for the Euroleague alone, where games are generally scheduled only two per week—a third to half of those played in a WNBA season. That, the pay, and the overall lifestyle certainly can be enticing.

The European league also benefits from the fact that opposing teams are relatively close to one another, making travel to away games less fatiguing than in the United States. Travel in the Euroleague can also be adventurous. Especially through tournament games, Lindsay has become a worldwide sightseer, visiting countries from Mexico and Brazil to Spain, France, Germany and Switzerland. Croatia was one of her favorites.

"We got to go out on the sea in boats," she says of her free time there. "It's an awesome place. Really beautiful."

Those who take on the challenge of playing in both leagues often return to the WNBA as better players. The variety of styles and the new plays they learn, along with the challenge of adapting to international rules, sharpens not only physical skills but mental acuity. The refereeing is also different, and overall game play is more demanding. That suits the lightening fast and acrobatic Lindsay Whalen just fine. The way to handle working the back-to-back seasons, she says, is to rest and recharge as much as possible on the breaks between coming and going. Usually there is a gap of several weeks, sometimes a month, depending on tournament participation on either end.

The Euroleague has a limit of two Americans per team, but through various games Lindsay comes in contact with many familiar players from the States. In her first season overseas, playing in Russia for the UMMC (Urals Mining and Manufacturing Company) team, her American teammate was Detroit Shock forward Cheryl Ford, a familiar opponent from their WNBA days. But it didn't take long to get to know the European players and coaches, all of whom Lindsay quickly admired. The adaptability she had gained while in Connecticut proved useful, and her time in Europe contributed to a new maturity. That year the team did well, advancing to the Euroleague's eighth Finals. For her part, Lindsay averaged 9.1 points, 4.2 rebounds, and 2.1 assists.

In 2007, newly married Lindsay was off to Prague six days after her wedding to begin the first of her annual seasons playing for the ZVVC USK Praha team. Prague has now become her second home, and she looks forward to returning each year, even more so when Ben can come with her.

She's learned some phrases of the Czech language, many having to do with game plays. An interpreter, though, is always on hand for her and others during practices and games to help decipher commands. It has never been a huge issue for her since many players from English-speaking countries participate. But when needed, they've all devised ways to communicate with one another across language barriers.

Out on her own alone or with friends, Lindsay manages in the city with a small arsenal of words, although again, many of the locals speak English. She loves to tour the streets in her free time and is fascinated by the centuries-old architecture. Over time she's discovered favorite local cafés, and by the time her parents made their first visit she'd become familiar enough with the city to give them a tour.

Her dad, Neil, had been able to visit her in Russia, but this was the first trip to Prague for both him and her mom, Kathy. During their ten days with Lindsay and Ben, they took in as many sights as they could and grew to love the city as much as their daughter and son-in-law did.

"There's so much history there," explains Kathy. "We don't have that in the States. It's just fascinating to see centuries-old buildings and statues. Other parts are very colorful, lots of interesting painted buildings. It's the only city in the region that wasn't bombed in either of the world wars. We crossed the Charles Bridge and were told some scenes in *Mission Impossible* were filmed on it. It's all just so beautiful. The cathedral was magnificent, the castle, everything was."

Lindsay and her parents in Prague.

St. Vitus Cathedral is the biggest cathedral in the country and can be seen from miles away. It's situated in the Castle District, connected by the Charles Bridge to the neighborhood known as Old Town Prague. The cathedral has sections dedicated to various kings and saints, and the castle itself still houses the Czech Republic's government.

"We took a few guided tours, which were really informative for me, too," says Lindsay. "Almost too much information to take in, though. Prague has such a rich history, and even its newer sections are cool."

For anyone planning a European vacation, Lindsay would highly recommend adding Prague to the itinerary. She suggests seeing, among other features, the Astronomical Clock in the Old Town Square. It's a huge medieval clock that keeps track of sun and moon positions, has animated statues of the Apostles and other sculptures that appear hourly, an Old Czech time scale that runs by noting sunsets, a Zodiacal ring, and a modern-day monthly calendar. For a watch, it's pretty exquisite.

Lindsay's parents were able to see her play during their trip and were encouraged to see that her unique style had remained intact in an unfamiliar league. It was a style that served her well. By the end of the season she'd helped her team take fifth place in their group, averaging 14.9 points, 5.7 rebounds, and 3.6 assists a game—good enough to earn her a two-year extension on her contract under coach Lubor Blazek.

"He's great, as a coach and a person," she says. "He gets along with everybody on the team and we have a lot of admiration for him. I'm really happy to have the chance to work with him again."

During that season she was elected to play in the Euroleague All-Star game in March. A selection of the world's top players was divided into two teams, Europe and The Rest of the World. Lindsay was on the latter and selected by fan vote to be a starter. The game had a 24-player combined roster with four coaches chosen on the basis of their records in qualifying rounds. Played in Moscow, it was a high-scoring game with a halftime mixed couples shootout for entertainment—a big hit with the crowd. Europe ended up taking the electrifying game by a lop-sided 111-86 margin.

Of playing in an All-Star game, Lindsay says, "It's such a huge honor. The chance to play with some of the world's best players in a competition like this is an experience of a

lifetime. The fans are amazing, and it's so good to see all that support for women's basketball on an international level. I'll never forget that game."

The next year Lindsay was voted onto the team again for a game held in Paris. A sold out crowd greeted the teams, on which WNBA players were well represented. Lindsay stole the limelight in the first period with her unselfish play and 9 points; then it was Sylvia Fowles' turn to wow the fans with a one-handed dunk following a steal. Becky Hammon was voted MVP, finishing with 24 points, and also won the halftime three-point shooting contest. The outstanding play of everyone on both teams insured that the crowd got the show they'd come to see.

Meanwhile, the regular 2008–2009 Euroleague season was in full swing, and Lindsay was enjoying life on and off the court. She continued to pick up the local language plus

A promo display of Lindsay (left) with Prague teammates Marketa Bednarova, Sandra Le Drean, and Ivanka Matic.

bits of several others through her contact with players from all over the world." She had grown accustomed to the arena, the city, and her surroundings, having spent roughly half of each of the previous four years there.

Her apartment the first two years in Prague had been in an older-style complex that had its inconveniences, including a small refrigerator and an antiquated heater on the wall in the bathroom instead of a clothes dryer. The heater had two racks, one of which pulled down from the ceiling. Lindsay went through several pairs of socks a day, and a few pairs were always drying on one rack or the other. In the fall of the next season, 2009, she requested—and got—a more modern, three-bedroom apartment for her and Ben, not only bigger but closer to her practice and play.

Living in Prague has allowed both of them to appreciate more fully the luxuries and conveniences we have in the United States. For example, in Prague, the recycling bins are placed in centralized spots, the closest of which is a block from their third floor apartment. Lindsay and Ben actually find themselves walking quite a bit. Though the team issued Lindsay a car, parking is an ever-present issue, as it is in most major cities. In her first year in Prague, she was given a car with a manual transmission, which she had no idea how to drive. The car looked wonderful sitting there with her name and the team's name on it, but since Ben hadn't arrived yet to teach her how it worked, it was a matter of just looking at it or become a fast learner through trial and error. She proceeded with no major fender-benders.

Until she and Ben got BlackBerrys, it was rather difficult to communicate or keep up with friends, family, and news from back home. The BlackBerrys made a huge difference, and Ben's setup of a Slingbox connection further helped them to stay in touch and informed—and watch Vikings games!—on television via the Internet.

The end of the 2009 season saw Lindsay's USK Praha team reached the play-offs, with she and fellow All-Star Evanthia Maltsi both awarded new contracts for the upcoming year. The team placed fourth in their group, having lost in the eighth finals to Russia. Lindsay averaged 15.4 points, 6.4 rebounds and 3.3 assists a game that year.

During her latest overseas season to date, 2009–2010, Lindsay once again was voted onto the All-Star roster, with the play this time in Gdynia, Poland, on March 9th.

Alongside her on the Rest of The World team was DeLisha Milton, power forward for Ros Casares Valencia, a team that would later knock ZVVZ USK Prague out of contention in the first round of the Euroleague play-offs. It was an otherwise strong season for the Prague team, which not only reached the Euroleague Women's post-season but also won the Czech Cup in a nail-biting 99-96 finale over Frisco Siko Brno, making them the first team in over a decade to wrestle the cup from that perennial champion.

At the end of the season Lindsay had impressive averages of 15.6 points, 4.8 rebounds and 2.7 assists per game. She was happy with her play, and as always, with the team, her coach, and the city.

"The Euroleague is an amazing opportunity," she adds. "It's just a matter of finding a good fit. I think Prague just fits me."

She'll be returning for a fifth year in the Euroleague, albeit with some changes in her life. While the past season was in progress, she was also on the roster for the USA Women's Basketball's team, opening a bid for an Olympic placement. And midway through the European tour came news of where she would play in her next WNBA season. It was a good year for Lindsay, hands down.

10

USA Basketball:
The Women's National Team

The United States women's national basketball team is composed of the top women players drawn from both college and professional teams. They are the defending Olympic champions, and have won the gold at the last four Olympic games.

Lindsay's first encounter with the team was when she played against them during her 2004 WNBA rookie season. She was selected to the WNBA All-Star squad that year, and was chosen by fan vote to be a starter. Due to Olympic scheduling, the game was held at Radio City Music Hall in New York. The USA team beat the WNBA All-Stars convincingly, 74 to 58.

"It was such a huge honor," Lindsay later remarked, "and the fan vote meant so much too. Other than our team getting beat as bad as we did, it was a great time and fun to be playing there. It's quite an impressive place and the whole thing was really something I'll never forget."

There had been very little practice time—just one day, in fact, making it difficult to find a rhythm or set up plays. Nevertheless the All Stars did their best against some of the best players in the world. From these games between top notch players, both newcomers to the USA round and seasoned veterans, are drawn the players that comprise the USA Olympic team. Lindsay didn't make it that year, but she was young yet in basketball years and experience, and there would be other chances. A few weeks later the US women's team was on its way to the Summer Olympics in Athens where they took home a much-deserved gold medal.

The Radio City Music Hall game was Lindsay's first as a WNBA All-Star, but she'd been selected in previous years to play on the national team as a collegiate All-American selection. In 2002 she was a member of the USA World Championship for Young Women Qualifying Team under 20 which emerged from the international tournament in Brazil with a 4-0 record and a gold medal. In 2003 she was again selected to play for the United States, this time in the under 21 bracket. Their record that year was 7-1 which gave them the gold again at the competition in Croatia.

Those games came during the summer off-season, complimenting the fall-through-spring sweep of the college basketball year. The WNBA season, on the other hand, runs from spring through fall, opposite the NBA season. Lindsay's 2004 All-Star game fell midway through her first season with the Connecticut Sun, giving her a very busy introduction to the world of professional sports.

In recent years the USA Basketball Women's National

Team has dominated in international competition, winning four consecutive Olympic gold medals (1996, 2000, 2004, 2008) and sporting a 63-1 record, with two gold medals in FIBA World Championships, one bronze, and one FIBA Americas Championship gold. Clearly, for an American player to join the USA team would be a huge honor.

In 2007 Lindsay received that honor, scoring 10 points in an 80-56 quarterfinal win in Australia which helped the team on their way to a 4-0 record. Next up was the 2007 FIBA zone championships. The FIBA (which stands for Fédération Internationale de Basketball) was established in Switzerland in 1957 as a governing body for world basketball. The top teams from the Americas zone met in Valdivia, Chile, in September of 2007. Competing against the United States that year were Argentina, Brazil, Canada, Chile, Cuba, Jamaica, and Mexico.

The US team once again won the gold medal with a 19-0 record. In March 2008, the team resumed its Olympic training at tournaments in Salamanca and Valencia, Spain. In Valencia, they played against Euroleague team Ros Casares, ranked No. 1 in the Spanish League, and in Salamanca against Perfumerias Avenida, ranked No. 2.

Among the players joining Lindsay as members of the USA Basketball Women's National Team were Seimone Augustus and Lindsey Harding, both at that time with the Minnesota Lynx, and her former Gopher teammate, Janel McCarville, now playing during the regular season with the New York Liberty team.

But only twelve members of the USA team could be

included on 2008 Olympic team. Nine of the choices had already been made—Seimone Augustus, Katie Smith, Lisa Leslie, Tina Thompson, Diana Taurasi and Sue Bird, Cappie Pondexter, Sylvia Fowles, and Candace Parker. That left three spots to be filled. Two forwards were soon picked—DeLisha Milton-Jones and Tamika Catchings. Though Lindsay was in the running right up to the end, the final spot finally went to guard Kara Lawson.

"It would have been really nice to make it," Lindsay says. "But I'm honored to have been on the roster and to play with such talented players…. It's such an honor to even be listed with them."

Later that year the US team brought home their fourth consecutive Olympic gold medal.

In 2009 organizers were already looking ahead to the 2012 games, and Lindsay was once again invited to the U.S. Women's Fall Training Camp that September by the five-member USA selection committee. But just weeks before the camp's scheduled start, she injured her eye while playing with Connecticut in a game against Indiana, and though she attended the session, she was unable to participate. She was still out in October when the USA team won three games in a row on their way to winning the 2009 UMMC Ekaterinburg International Invitational Tournament.

"It was too bad to be out," Lindsay reflected, speaking of both events. "The camp and the invitational give players a chance to see how to work as a team. A point guard has to know how a team moves and plays in order to set up the best position for shots, so it's hard to miss out on that. I've played with injuries before, but with my eye, it's different. I really had to be very careful to make sure it healed properly."

The following spring Lindsay was once again absent from the training sessions of the national team, this time due to conflicts with her Euroleague season in Prague, but when the official 2010–2012 USA National Team roster was announced in March, she was among the chosen twenty, twelve of whom will eventually represent the USA in the 2010 World Championships and the 2012 Olympics.

Lindsay is hopeful that this time she'll make the final roster, feeling that she has more to offer than last time around. "I think my previous experience playing with the national team will help. It also should help that I've been playing in Europe for the past four seasons and have gotten familiar with the international rules and styles. Hopefully those things will make me a better player now than when I was younger."

The announcement, made just after the 2010 regular season trades, reunited Lindsay with former and upcoming teammates. The nineteen other candidates were: Seimone Augustus and Candice Wiggins (Minnesota Lynx), Renee Montgomery, Kara Lawson and Asjha Jones (Connecticut Sun), Lindsey Harding and Alana Beard (Washington Mystics), Diana Taurasi and Candice Dupree (Phoenix Mercury), Tina Charles and Maya Moore (University of Connecticut), Sue Bird and Swin Cash (Seattle Storm), Candace Parker (Los Angeles Sparks), Cappie Pondexter and Shameka Christon (New York Liberty), Angel McCoughtry (Atlanta Dream), Tamika Catchings (Indiana Fever), and Sylvia Fowles (Chicago Sky).

Twelve of the players chosen already have experience on gold medal teams, and six others, including Lindsay, were on the 2007–2008 USA Women's National Team. Most of the players are already familiar with the team coach, Geno Auriemma, who is also head coach of the University of Connecticut Huskies, having played either with him or against him at some time in their collegiate careers. And he, in turn, knows most of the players, which will make his coaching job that much easier. Auriemma served as assistant coach for the U.S. Olympic Team in 2000, and looks forward to qualifying for the 2012 Olympic Games in London at the upcoming 2010 FIBA World Championship Games, which are scheduled for September 23rd to October 3rd, 2010 in Brno, Karlovy Vary, and Ostrava, all in the Czech Republic.

That gold medal winner will have earned a berth in the Olympics, but it isn't the only way to qualify. Two more chances would come at the 2011 FIBA Americas Olympic Qualifying Tournament and again in 2012 at the FIBA World Olympic Qualifying Tournament. Only time will tell how the US team will do. For Lindsay, to play on the Olympic team would be a career highlight.

"It definitely would be great," she says. "I think my chances are pretty good. But so are everybody's. We just have to keep playing the best we can and see what happens."

11

THE LYNX LINK-UP

January 12, 2010. The Minnesota Lynx were ecstatic, and so was Lindsay, despite her affection and gratitude for all things Connecticut. She was coming home to her state team and family.

The Lynx had finally completed the trade they'd been eager to make for six years. The deal gave them Lindsay and a second round draft pick. In exchange, Connecticut got the top overall pick, along with former U of Connecticut point guard Renee Montgomery to fill Lindsay's spot.

The abiding affection that Lynx fans felt for Lindsay had been unmistakable throughout the six seasons she was in Connecticut. Every time they played against the Sun, crowds flocked to the game for a sight of the Whalen floor magic. The 2004 match, her first WNBA appearance in Minnesota, broke all attendance records for a Lynx game with 16,227 showing up to watch their home-state girl. At every such Lynx-Sun match-up since, her maneuvers brought deafening cheers despite the fact those plays gave the Sun the advantage.

Undeniably, Minnesota wanted Lindsay back home.

Not only did her street-smart flair and skillful finesse draw crowds, she was loved for who she was. The fact she had started 196 of 197 games for the Sun and averaged at least 10 points, 5 rebounds, and 5 assists per game throughout that span of time (one of only two players to accomplish the feat) was frosting on the cake.

The deal was actually initiated by the Sun as part of a strategy to bring center Tina Charles, a recent U of Connecticut alum, into the fold. Coach Thibault considered this a key move for the team, and it was the critical factor in his decision to pursue the trade. The Sun were willing to give up their star point guard because they'd be getting another point guard, Renee Montgomery, in return, as well as the coveted top overall pick that would allow them to draft Charles. To round out their revised team, they went after free agent Kara Lawson and also got her. So the Lindsay trade was a definite win for the Sun as well as for Minnesota.

Lindsay was in the Czech Republic finishing her season for USK Prague at the time of the announcement and got the news via both her agent and the team.

"I was really excited about the chance to play at home," she said. "For a lot of reasons. Of course, my family is there, so is Ben's. Minnesota is the best, it's home. But this is about basketball. I think the team is strong with a lot of talent and will be a great team to be a part of. Would be really great to go for the top spot with them in the Western Conference."

She adds that ever since she turned pro, playing for the Lynx had been somewhere in the back of her mind. The fact that it worked out this year is amazing to her, and though she was anxious to go, the off-season before the actual transition brought a mix of emotions to the surface.

"During those four months until I actually was going home," she says, "I was thrilled but there were some sad parts. When you're on a team, you're all for the team. I loved them and the coaches and being part of it all. So it was sad to say goodbye."

When asked for her thoughts on not playing for the Lynx six years ago, right out of college, Lindsay responds, "I'm fine with that, really. It's right. It went the way it was supposed to."

She means it. Her years with Connecticut gave her much-needed experience, not just as a player but as a person. It also gave her time to sort out how those two aspects of a professional career combine to create a new maturity. Starting a professional career with a home team, especially in light of the popularity she'd developed as a college star, would have presented Lindsay with a variety of added pressures that might have hindered or delayed her skill development. No, she's fine with the way things went.

The Lynx are hoping her throng of fans, many of whom expressed vehement disapproval of the team for not trying harder to bring her on board immediately following her years as a Gopher, have come to feel the same way Lindsay does about it. It wasn't that the Lynx hadn't tried. But their draft pick wasn't high enough that year and Connecticut got to her first. In subsequent years, they entered into trade talks with the Sun, but according to Roger Griffith, the team's

Lindsay addresses the fans on her return to Minnesota.

executive vice president, the ransom Connecticut was asking in return for their star would have jeopardized the whole Minnesota franchise. As badly as they wanted her, it just wasn't feasible.

In an interesting twist of fate, new Lynx coach Cheryl Reeve also had her eye on Lindsay at that time. As assistant coach for the Detroit Shock, she scouted her frequently. Now that Coach Reeve is with the Lynx, she couldn't be more pleased to have Lindsay on the roster.

Judging by the overwhelming media coverage at the acquisition announcement, it seems the news of Lindsay finally returning is what the public in Minnesota had hungered to hear. Modest as ever, Lindsay herself is a bit surprised her legacy hasn't faded during her six-year absence—a long time in the sporting world.

"It's so cool to know that people care, that they're

excited," she says. "I always kind of hoped this would happen in the back of my mind, that I'd come back here to play. I'm ready for the season to get started, even if it's all still a little surreal."

On her mind now is pleasing those fans, herself, and the franchise by giving it her all.

"You play better when there are expectations. We all do. We all try to improve our individual games the best we can. The only way to go for playoffs, a championship, is to earn it by proving we deserve it. What people want is a great game on the floor."

She's right, although her role-model status brings expectations off the floor too—ones she's not only aware of but does her best to honor.

In joining the Lynx, Lindsay becomes the team's fifth player with All-Star status on the current roster, along with Charde Houston (Connecticut), Seimone Augustus (Louisiana State), Rebekkah Runson (Georgetown), and Nicky Anosike (Tennessee). Gifted newcomer Monica Wright (Virginia) joins the existing talent of Candice Wiggins (Stanford), Quanitra Hollingsworth (Virginia Commonwealth), Hamchetou Maiga-Ba (Old Dominion), Nuria Martinez (Spain), and Rashanda McCants (North Carolina) to round out the team.

With so many stars on the Lynx already, Lindsay dismisses her new 'face of the team' status in favor of emphasizing the importance of team effort. She is not oblivious to her popularity, and is thrilled it draws crowds to the games, but prefers to concentrate on her plays and her part on the team. It's an attitude that has made her the player she is, and greatly contributes to her fans' fascination with her.

She has also been welcomed by her new teammates. Charde Houston, who plays forward for the Lynx and also played with Lindsay last winter in Prague, has high praise, noting that Lindsay has the ability to maximize the team's talents by her outstanding floor leadership. And Seimone Augustus, who herself has been the face of the Lynx since joining the team in 2006, actually kidded Lindsay back in October at trials for the USA women's basketball team in Washington, DC, telling her she'd be such a great addition to the team, which was really shaping into a contender. Neither she nor Lindsay knew at the time how quickly such a turn of events would transpire!

Lindsay brings the ball up court in a game against Seattle, July 17, 2010.

With such talent and team spirit, the Lynx, projected in a preseason poll of general managers to be the league's most improved team, are well on their way to being that.

At the same time, although playing is paramount, Lindsay also approached Lynx executive Gordon Smith when she first arrived in town and committed to doing as much as she could to promote the team. Sponsors had already been jumping onboard. She volunteers her time without pay, per team policy, but that doesn't negate the effectiveness or desire of Lindsay and other players to contribute their effort for the sake of the sport's betterment. They do so because they understand the overall game. In the end, it's not about personal popularity or great plays for the sake of those things alone—it's about enticing the crowds who pay the ticket money that supports the game directly; these paying customers, in turn, lure sponsors who also do their part in footing the bill, the end result being that the sport continues to thrive. It's the game inside the games of sport.

Bringing in Lindsay helped renew sponsorships from corporations such as U.S. Bank, Verizon, Target, and Best Buy. Then there's Gold 'n Plump, the fresh chicken distributor, who has enlisted Lindsay as game-spot spokesperson, filming video segments of her cooking healthy recipes with their Minnesota-raised product. Lindsay is also doing in-arena promotions for Explore Minnesota and for the Girl Scouts, who rightfully see Lindsay as a fitting role model.

Then there's the merchandising. Throughout her career Lindsay has been immortalized in buttons, posters, bobble-heads, [#]13 tees and jerseys, and commemorative hologram cards. Contests with giveaways and free gifts at game doors add to the joy of her fans and team. Such mementoes provide immediate revenue but are no less important as visible reminders of her enduring popularity.

Less obvious merchandising comes in the form of personal appearances—publicity which earlier in her career made Lindsay uncomfortable. Along with press conferences and interviews, there are appearances at luncheons and autograph signings at the Mall of America and the Ronald McDonald House. In May she was called upon to throw out the ceremonial first pitch of the Yankees-Twins game at the Target Center, an appearance that underscored her role as a home state hero whose appeal transcends the borders between sports. It was definitely an honor, and it also brought a burst of publicity for her own sport.

But nothing generates excitement and draws crowds more than winning. And those same great crowds who pay also nobly serve to spur on a team, to energize it and give it reason to pull out all the stops. Their cheers matter. The roar for an exquisite play is felt and shared by the whole team like a bolt of lightning, taking them with new zest to the next play, the next shot, the next score, and ultimately the win. Winning feeds on itself by bringing a team to the play-offs, which attracts fans, revenue, higher salaries and better players, increasing a team's chances of winning the next season.

The hope for the Lynx, with the line-up now in place, is to win the Western Conference and compete for the WNBA Final. It may take time for the players to adjust to one another and develop a rhythm as a team, but the goal is still and always unequivocally to reach the top. And it's much more probable with Lindsay on the roster than ever before in the Lynx's eleven-year history. In that time they've only qualified for the postseason twice and have never won a playoff series.

Yes, it's about numbers and money and winning, yet the deal with Connecticut to get Lindsay carried added meaning for many Minnesota sports fans. She is the embodiment of all they stand for in values, in demeanor, in zest and zeal. She recognized her talent and honed it and used it and sacrificed to perfect it. Her rise to fame was completely her own doing. Minnesotans, and many, many others, see in her what they hope to someday find in themselves, even those who are past their prime. There's always a way and time to be the best you can be. That's what people see in Lindsay.

And in Minnesota they have worked hard to make sure she knows that. Her home town of Hutchinson, in conjunction with the Lynx, began formulating celebration plans the day of the draft announcement. Soon an exciting series of events to honor Lindsay's return took shape.

Friday, May 7, 2010, was proclaimed "Lindsay Whalen Day" by Steve Cook, Hutchinson's mayor. He opened ceremonies on that day to a packed crowd at the City Center in town, emceed by John Mons, station manager of local KDUZ radio. Lindsay was greeted with applauding cheers from assembled fans befitting the royal place she holds in their hearts. Featured speakers took the floor to recount memories, expound on their admiration, and toast Lindsay's future career.

Coach Andy Rostberg from Hutchinson High took the stage, reliving for the crowd Lindsay's glory days at Hutchinson High. More speakers followed, all sharing anecdotes about Lindsay's high school years and expressing their pride in all she has accomplished since that time. Next Lindsay came onstage to appreciative applause, thanked everyone, took questions and signed autographs. Then she was off to St. Anastasia Elementary School to greet her youngest fans and share memories with them of her days in the very same classrooms.

The next stop was the Hutchinson Orthopedic & Fracture Clinic where Lindsay visited with pediatric and adult therapy patients. Dinner at Zella's Restaurant came next, then more autograph signing, before Lindsay and her entourage returned to the Events Center to oversee some of the HYBA sponsored youth hoops shooting contests and games. The evening concluded with music, food, and prizes. Lynx apparel and bus tickets were sold for a caravan to games. It was a fitting and joyous occasion.

Two days later, Lindsay turned a mere twenty-eight.

Hutchinson is indeed proud. They probably would have been proud had she become just a middling player. But she didn't, she became a phenom, which explains why her appeal and adoration extends far beyond the city limits of Hutchinson, beyond the borders of Minnesota and the United States. Over the years she has continued to exhibit the personal qualities that originally made her a standout. She's grounded; she's sincerely humble, acknowledging that the fuss and attention often surprises her. She's a homebody at heart, happy to be

close to her family and Ben's, to settle into a familiar setting surrounded by the people she knows well.

As her former Gopher coach Pam Borton said of her recently, "It's so easy for players to let success change them. She's one in a million because she hasn't let that happen."

Connecticut coach Thibault agrees, adding that she's the kind of player who grows with every game, continually on the alert to improve. She's becoming a better shooter and a better defender with each season, and he feels that she has not yet reached her peak.

Both coaches have watched Lindsay entertain the crowds with her finesse, her expertise, her creative no-look passes and spinning drives. Lindsay has a street-savvy instinct to get the job done whether it means passing or going for a risky 3-pointer, and that quality has enthralled fans ever since she was a teen. It comes naturally to her, but to say it comes easily would be to ignore the long hours of practice and study involved.

Her growth has come in all areas. Early in her career, as much as she excelled at the sport even then, she found talking about it to the media less than natural. Now she's more relaxed, can ad lib with the best of them, and reads off a teleprompter when needed without missing a beat. She has accomplished it through practice, realizing such proficiency is needed in her stature as a role model.

Her sense of humor shows through easily now, dry as it is, while she's still reserved and rather quiet by nature. It carries to the floor during games, even when she unleashes the aggression that gets the job done. She is an electrifying joy to watch. The public preoccupation with her is deserved and makes perfect sense. She's showing us how to live by the grace she employs under pressure, by the calm yet steadfast determination in her face. She's polite, she's kind, she's all about team. She loves her sport with every fiber of her being. She is a sportswoman with a burning desire to see women's sports be valued, and is accomplishing that through her character and by playing with her whole heart and soul.

That is the value of her to the Lynx. They have the same goal. The idea of winning and drawing fans isn't for a game, a season; it's to create lifelong followers for the future of women in professional basketball. It's vital for a league still so young, and one who has dwindled from 16 teams to twelve. Beyond the fact she's a fabulous point guard rests the issue of what she can do for the next generation of women,

the chance she may keep open for them the chance to succeed as she has.

Why is that so important? The very same drive that propels young men to test their physical abilities is shared equally by young women. Both men and women need the opportunity athletics offers to enrich their lives through training, endurance, and skill-refinement. Athletics provides both men and women the experience of winning and losing, of individual excellence, team-building, sacrifice, and fair-play. Athletics contribute to their development not only as athletes but as leaders, workers, parents, and citizens who contribute to society in constructive ways.

That all-embracing equality is also important for fans young and old, who crave the enrichment that comes from watching and vicariously sharing in athletic feats that push limits, stretch boundaries, and go beyond what is thought of as humanly possible. To witness such events gives us hope, renews our spirit, shows us the beauty of inner and outer strength. Watching such events also gives us the pure fun of distraction from the mundane and prods us into doing better. Into believing in the impossible.

Not too long ago, slightly before Lindsay's time, the only athletic outlet for girls in school was a fifty-minute physical education class three times a week. The advancement has been good. It has a ways to go.

Women's sports have given us Lindsay Whalen. That's as good a reason as any to support them. And Lindsay, in turn, is doing what she can to ensure that the upcoming generation of young girls, and those to follow, have the same opportunities she had. She'd like that for their sake and for the ongoing enrichment the advance offers to fans.

12

POINTS TO GUARD:

AN INTERVIEW WITH LINDSAY

In answering the following questions, Lindsay shares her personal thoughts on her own career as they might hopefully apply and strengthen the passion and perseverance in other aspiring young people, and even the not so young.

ON FINDING YOUR PASSION

Question: How did you know basketball was for you?

Lindsay: I think it was the first time I played in a real game, when I made that shot from the side of the backboard. I just had so much fun playing, and I really enjoyed being on a team. Other than hockey with boys and a little soccer, I'd never had that. I just loved the game and my grade school best friends were on that team. It just kind of went from there. I started practicing at home after that shot. It didn't come easy right away, but I could tell I had an itch for it.

Question: Can you define the elements of basketball that enticed you the most?

Lindsay: I would say the competition and being part of a team, having them as friends, which, going into college and then the pros. becomes even more important. Everyone has to be on the same page to work the game plan, and it helps if we all know everyone's objective on the court. I think just having all of that in focus is a great feeling, then to go out and do it. So it's the competition and the team camaraderie that I like.

Question: What would you suggest to someone who just doesn't have the talent for a certain sport or goal but still wants to try?

Lindsay: I would say there are a lot of things, especially in sports, that you can get really good at if you work hard at them. Growing up, I saw a lot of players who had the talent to play in college or in the WNBA, but they didn't work at it or didn't dedicate themselves. And I've see a lot of players in the WNBA now who aren't as talented as some I saw in college, but they worked and got good at a couple of particular things that the team needed, or they were a really great teammate, or someone that other people in the organization wanted to have around because they knew what it took to win. It's not always the talented person who wins or gets picked for a team, because there are so many things in basketball, or any sport, that you can offer a team. You'll get your shot but you have to be willing to put the effort in and the energy to make that possible. If it was easy everybody would be doing it, but the reason only some make it to certain levels in sports is because they're willing to work hard.

Question: What are the signs a person has hit on the right thing?

Lindsay: Once you find out what you're getting good at or what you want to do, what your calling is, I think you realize that you just know. That's after you've put in the time and have seen the hard work pay off in any field. For me in basketball, it was in college when we started winning my sophomore year, or maybe when I got drafted—certain things along the way show you this is the right decision you've made, the right thing to be doing. When you have a good game or you're doing well at something—and that doesn't need to mean someone else complimenting you—you just have that knack or self-confidence that what you're doing is the right thing.

Question: Did you have a mentor who helped you?

Lindsay: I had a lot of them. My parents, of course, and all of my coaches, like Andy Rostberg in high school. Andy really helped me look toward college, too. Then Pam Borton in college. She was my coach for two years and taught me how to play defense. She made me realize I had to play both ends of the court to make it to the pros. I'd known that before but to have somebody put it like she did and really stress it was big for me. And then Coach Thibault in Connecticut, who taught me how to be professional, how to play best point guard. I played for him for six years and he taught me so much. They're all important because you spend so much time with them. Anything you can learn from them you need to take in. Now this year with Coach Reeve, it's the same thing, just learning from her. It's great having different coaches and different perspectives to learn from, so I've been really fortunate throughout the years having them as mentors.

Question: Is it alright to give up if you find you don't like something?

Lindsay: Yeah, but what I would say is, if you don't like something, if you don't have a true passion for it, that's not quitting, it's just knowing that it wasn't for you. If you're not having fun doing something, you know it. Ben has always told me, and my parents have too, that if basketball ever stops being fun or stops being something I have a passion for, then it's probably time to look for something else. And I wouldn't say that if I stopped, it'd be quitting. You have to love what you do in order to be successful at it. I've been playing a long time and still have a passion for it so I keep playing. I think that goes for people in a lot of lines of work. You're not always going to love your job every day, it's not always going to be great, but I think there always has to be that certain element. You need it even outside of work because that's what makes anything worthwhile.

Question: If a person is good at several things, is it necessary to choose one?

Lindsay: I get this question a lot from junior athletes at camps because girls at fourteen, fifteen, sixteen are playing tennis, basketball, softball, and wondering if they have to choose one. I think when you get to a certain age, probably in college, if you're going to play sports you should probably choose to play just one, but up until your junior or senior year of high school, play as many sports as you can. I feel like I got a lot of my coordination and athletic ability playing so many sports. It helps in getting that hand-eye coordination and learning how to be on different teams and have different coaches. Eventually if you come down to one sport, those skills are going to help you in it. You can take everything you learned in all of them and put that energy into it. Another reason is that playing a variety will help you decide which one you really want.

Question: Can obstacles be a good thing?

Lindsay: That's how everybody gets to where they are. That's how I've gotten to where I am. Everyone does, everyone has had things they've had to work on that definitely just make them stronger. In college I had three coaches in three years and each year we had to not only get to know a new coach but learn a new system. Then there are always players transferring out from the team and others coming in, it all really helped make us stronger and learn how to adjust. I remember, this is way back now, the first time I had to go to overnight camp in like seventh or eighth grade. I wanted to come home and called my parents crying after just one day. I didn't want to stay, but then after like the third day I was loving it and kind of coming out from my shell. I had to adjust, and I think that's the kind of thing that makes you the person you are today, in sports or anything.

Question: What are some of the personal benefits of having gone for your goal?

Lindsay: Well, everything happens for a reason anyway, it seems, but I never would have met Ben if we both hadn't earned scholarships to Minnesota, and now we're married. I've also gotten to see so much of the world. I've gotten to live in Prague for four years and I lived in Russia. I'd taken probably four or five trips to Europe even before I lived there for national teams and junior teams because I was achieving goals and making those teams. I've met so many people and made so many friends, so I've just had a lot of great experiences. My parents have gotten to go to Europe, my whole family got to come to Connecticut a couple of times. I look back at my ten years or so in basketball and all it's been able to do for me, all because I'd gone for goals and wanted to earn the scholarship and to play in the WNBA and compete for the national team. All those things have brought me just great experiences and taken me to places I'd never otherwise gotten to see.

Question: You obviously love what you do but have been known to often wear a scowl during a game. Can you explain that?

Lindsay: It's just intensity, being in the moment of the game. You get so into it and want to win so badly that it just happens.

People tell me that I should smile more and look like I'm having fun. I am having fun, but then something little won't go right or I know I should have done something else and I just get that intensity frown. It's just part of me trying to think about what I'm doing, but I still feel like I'm usually having fun in spite of doing that look.

Question: How does it feel to be fulfilling your chosen passion?

Lindsay: It feels like … I don't know what word to use other than great. I mean, to be able to be playing basketball and doing it professionally is … again, great. That's the best word. Playing all the time growing up, then earning the scholarship, then to keep playing, it's been awesome. A lot of kids, I know not all but a lot, grow up wanting to be a professional athlete, to play at the highest level of sports. I've been able to do that and have that kind of success. It's great.

ON SUCCESS

Question: What would you say is the most important quality you have, or have fostered, that has helped you achieve success?

Lindsay: I would say I've really learned how to work hard. I've learned how to go at game speed even when I'm practicing, and I've learned how to put in time away from practice. I especially learned that in college, and I think putting in time on the off-season got me into the WNBA. I'm still working on individual things, and I've also learned in the last three or four years how to take better care of my body. At this point in my career I want to play yet for a number of years and to do that I need to do those kinds of things along the way. You learn that from people who are older than you, you watch what they do and you kind of go from there and try to do those things yourself.

Question: What does success mean to you?

Lindsay: I think the bottom line in pro sports comes down to the winning, but what that involves is being successful at improving as an individual and as a team. Success outside of basketball, sports, means being happy and enjoying your family, loving your family, that's what really counts in life. I think there are a couple of ways to define success but those are some for me. Enjoying what you're doing is success.

Question: What have been your successes besides basketball?

Lindsay: It's been being married to Ben, and having a close family life with my own brothers and sisters and getting to know his. I feel like a part of his family now. Also, doing the right thing and helping people when I can and giving back to my community. Anything a person can do to help out is a big thing. Being there for my brothers and sisters goes to a healthy family relationship which again, to me, is so important.

Question: Have you ever had any low periods or setbacks? If so, how did you handle them?

Lindsay: Well, my ankle surgery, for one. That was a setback where I couldn't play for four months. I couldn't walk without crutches for a month and a half, two months of that time. I had to come back and work myself into shape, then play when I probably wasn't a hundred percent. Then too, it happened when I was in Connecticut and Ben was tied up with his playing, although at one point I was able to go with him for a few days right before I started rehab. My family was back in Minnesota, and even though the Thibaults were just great it still was a pretty lonely time. But then being able to work through it and get back on the court and back to where I was when I was fine, I think is a good metaphor for handling a setback. There's actually something every season, there's never going to be a season go exactly as you've set it up. There's always going to be ups and downs but the more you stay the course, the more you try to stay as even as possible the better. You can't get too down or too up on yourself.

Question: How has basketball, and being part of a team, helped shape your character?

Lindsay: Besides the fact that being part of a team is fun, it offers a lot. The team camaraderie, having to work well with others—getting along with everyone on the court for sure—all being on the same page, that bond with people, it's priceless. The ability to understand where they're coming from, their background, how they think, helps you as a person because then you know what it takes to have a group of people come together to work for one thing. I think that makes each individual person a better person. That's why playing high school sports, junior high sports, is so important for kids because you learn how to interact with people and learn life lessons while also staying active.

Question: Can you describe the feeling of having made a perfect play?

Lindsay: Terrific. The other night I drove baseline and got a good pass to Seimone and she made the 3-point shot that was the winning basket. It went exactly the we drew it up in the timeout, it's what Coach wanted us to do. As point guard I made the pass, which was my main job to do. Then, while others were busy, Seimone got open and made the shot. We all worked together. It's just a great feeling, there's nothing like it, especially at the end of a game in that moment when you know the shot will probably make the win. It's not easy to do and doesn't always happen, but when it does it's a pretty big deal.

Question: How does it feel when a play goes awry?

Lindsay: For me it's usually a turnover, and there's that instant "shouda, woulda, coulda" thing, but as I've gotten older I've tried to quickly put it behind me because there's usually a lot of game left and other plays to make. You just have to get back on defense, or if a player scored on you then you get back on offense. The more you can get to the point of knowing it's over—that there'll be another play—the better you're going to be. You have to have a short memory because otherwise you can't get yourself back in the game.

Question: Do you ever personally take responsibility for a win? Loss?

Lindsay: No, I don't think anyone ever can. It's a team game, a team sport. Even if you've missed the last shot or free-throw, or made both, there are so many plays in a game that contribute to the end result. One quote my dad always told me was "share the credit, take the blame" because that's the way it works best.

Question: Is it difficult to leave the game behind you after it's over?

Lindsay: Sometimes. We usually take fifteen minutes to a half hour to go over things with the coach about what went well or should have gone better, then move on because there are so many games in a season, probably one within the following few days. It's part of sports, it's part of that competitive nature that got you involved, so a win is fantastic, a great feeling, and a loss is a let-down, a sting that's going to hurt. It's just the way it is. Whether we win or lose, the next day it's over and done with and the sun comes up for a new one. It's just something I've learned after so many years of playing. You just have to move forward, although it's sometimes easier said than done.

Question: You have been called extremely fun to watch. Aside from your intensely concentrating face, are you actually having fun during plays, or does it feel like work?

Lindsay: It's fun most of the time! It's got to be fun. It doesn't feel like work because I've been doing it since I was little, although of course there are times it's harder than others. It's my job but it's usually fun.

Question: Of all the memorabilia in your honor—posters, pins, the jerseys, the bobbleheads—do you have a favorite?

Lindsay: Let's see, I think the first bobblehead because I was the first athlete at the U to get one. That's pretty cool. And having my jersey retired. Both were really special honors.

ON WOMEN'S SPORTS

Question: You recently spoke at Pam Borton's Be a Champ Camp. Do you see any generational changes in these girls compared to when you began?

Lindsay: A lot of changes. There are more opportunities for girls to have a future in sports now, like in the WNBA or soccer, and there are professional athletes in those sports that they have a chance to look up to, something that I didn't have growing up. There's more technology. Everyone at the camp had a cell phone; they could take a cell phone picture and send it to friends. And it's amazing how the Internet offers so much information for them. It's a sign of the times, but it's also opened up so much for girls. They can go to these camps, play in AAU and tournaments, all things that I did too, but the opportunities are broader for them if they want to pursue sports. As for role models, my age group did have some ahead of us we could admire, and now we're able to do it for the upcoming ones in a bigger variety of sports. It's pretty cool that it keeps getting better all the time.

Question: You brought record attendance to games during your Gopher years. Can you explain the business ramifications of such attendance for the future of women in sports?

Lindsay: Doing well and filling up the stands means good money for a university. Basketball is one of the big revenue-generating sports. We loved doing so much for the university because it did so much for us. Bringing in those crowds helped them financially, so it was a great thing. It's a cycle. Having crowds means people are interested in the sport, and that means opportunity for the next generation. It also encourages that next generation. I mean, for young girls to come and see so many people watching, they're of course going to want to be down on that floor someday themselves. If you want to play, you want that experience for yourself. So crowd attendance is huge all the way around.

Question: Do you see women ever earning equal pay as men in sports?

Lindsay: No. I just don't see it happening, at least not any time soon. It won't happen until a women's sport can bring in the same kind of money. Football, baseball, those are America's pastimes, so is hockey. They're all men's sports. So is basketball, except we're gaining ground there. Tennis is probably the most equal for men and women. And women golfers can make pretty good money. There are other individual sports like figuring skating, too, but when it comes to team sports, overall, there's just a huge gap. NBA players make millions.

Question: Why, in your opinion, have women's sports taken a back seat to men's?

Lindsay: I think it's because women's sports are so relatively new. The WNBA, for instance, is only in its thirteenth or fourteenth year. Women's professional sports are still in their infancy. Football, baseball, hockey, golf, they've all been around almost forever and are such huge money-generating events, bringing in hundreds of thousands of fans. They're great entertainment—I watch them and love them myself. Still, I really think there's a niche and demand for women's sports, it's just going to take some more time.

Question: In what ways are women's sports vital?

Lindsay: To give young girls the same chance to aspire to sports as boys have. Sports are a hug part of our society and culture, in the world's culture for that matter, and for young girls to have the opportunity to work on their game and to earn a scholarship is huge. You have to have women's sports; it's just a necessity.

Question: What part do fans play?

Lindsay: Fans are the reason for our league, the WNBA. They love the game, love coming, and we love playing for them. Without the fans the sport wouldn't exist. Period!

Question: Can young girls themselves do anything to promote a sport in school?

Lindsay: Working hard and having a good team is the biggest thing. Winning and putting good players on the floor is key so people want to come and watch. That's what we did at the U. Fans wanted to watch us. That's the best promotion possible. You have to put the time in to be good and you have to be successful for sure.

Question: Are there ways to better finance sports for young girls?

Lindsay: It's hard to say. There probably are, I just don't know what they would be. It really comes down to just a growth in those sports so they bring in ticket sales. It's back to that cycle again of one encouraging the other. But they have to be given the chance, that's the beginning.

Question: Who are some of your heroes in women's sports?

Lindsay: I grew up watching Jennifer Capriati in tennis. I really liked her, and Carol Ann Shudlick, who played for the Gophers. I didn't get to watch many of Carol Ann's games growing up but when I did, it was great. Then there was Cynthia Cooper, Lisa Leslie, Tina Thompson, all the players I saw growing up were role models for me. And I really looked up to the older players on my high school basketball team. All of those were really influential for me.

Question: Do you see a bright future for women's sports?

Lindsay: I do. I think it can only get better. There are kids now working really hard on their games and having a good time being active in a lot of sports. So yes, definitely. They're getting better and better which means more wins and fans.

Question: What advice would you give to young players who hope to be successful in the game?

Lindsay: You have to work on your game outside of practice or required times. That's the biggest thing. If it's shooting on your garage backboard or wherever, you have to work at it. Just going to camps or playing on an AAU team isn't enough. You need to improve on your own. That's what I did. A lot of work on my own.

On Being Lindsay

Question: What is your favorite kind of music?

Lindsay: I like a lot of different kinds. Probably for basketball, I'd say hip-hop because that's what plays at the games. I also listen to classic rock, old rock, alternative rock. Not a whole lot of country except for Taylor Swift and Carrie Underwood, maybe a few more. Nothing too hard, I don't like hardcore heavy metal, but otherwise most everything that's on lately.

Question: Where did the nickname "DJ Whay" come from?

Lindsay: (Laughs) Actually, part of it, the DJ part, I gave myself in a way. I know not many people give themselves nicknames, but I give them to most everybody else, so it seemed fine. It just kind of came together after people started calling me "Whay"—short for Whalen. The DJ was because they always said in plays I would "spin around and drop a dime," so that basketball phrase just translated into DJ and stuck. There are quite a few people who still call me DJ Whay or some just DJ.

Question: Were you involved in high school extracurricular activities other than sports?

Lindsay: Not really, it was mainly just sports. I did belong to D.A.R.E., the group that helps keep kids from underage drinking, and also the FCA, the Fellowship of Christian Athletes. I was a part of that too.

Question: Do you and Ben share the same decorating taste?

Lindsay: Yeah, we do. Ben's really good at hanging things up, pictures and things. Actually he's really good, better than me at knowing where they should go. We're both pretty good at decorating and making sure the house looks nice, but he's the one who measures and makes sure things are centered— I'd be the one to just put something up, not sloppily but just not taking as much time to make sure it was right. He does that for us.

Question: Do you have any hidden talents?

Lindsay: I think I'm pretty good at making people laugh. It's probably the reason I'm good at leading in basketball, because

I try to keep things loose at critical times, which is good for people to have that chance to relieve stress. With Ben and my family and friends, I just like to make them laugh.

Question: What is it about Ben that told you he was the one?

Lindsay: Of course my feelings, then the fact we clicked, and then all the interests we had in common. We really enjoy doing the same things. We also are best friends, and I think that's what marriage is all about. We've had that from the start of our relationship, so that's the biggest thing that let me know.

Question: Do you and your teammates socialize outside of games?

Lindsay: Yeah, we do. We do a lot of going out to eat and hanging out, especially on the road. It's fun, it's being part of the team, and the time off-court is important because we work so hard when we're on it. This year in Minnesota, there's been a lot of laughing and being in good spirits so it's been an exceptionally fun year.

Question: How long do you plan to play each off-season in the Euroleague?

Lindsay: That depends on each year. I'm for sure signed for next year, then we'll take it year by year after that. So there's no real plans, it just always depends on how you're feeling, what the teams need, if Prague will offer me a contract again or if another team will, it all depends on those things. I also need to see how my body does, if the time off to rest between seasons is enough, so I'm just taking it one year at a time.

Question: Do you know what you'd have done career-wise if you hadn't gone into pro basketball?

Lindsay: My major was sports management, so I think I'd have been in advertising or marketing for a sports team. I've just always been a big sports fan, I guess a sports nut, so anything working with a sports team. Maybe coaching, but I think probably just working on the advertising, marketing end.

Question: Do you enjoy being asked for your autograph?

Lindsay: I do. I like signing things for people, especially young fans. Sometimes I'm rushed for time, like after a game when I should be getting back for post-game in the locker room, and I feel horrible saying no when I run past them. But I have to, and don't always have time to come back, unfortunately. At most other times and places, it's great.

Question: Would you describe your long-range plans and hopes for the future?

Lindsay: It's just what everybody wants for their future, just to be happy with whatever I'm doing, to be around family and friends, and to enjoy life and live it to the fullest.

On Being a Whole Person

Question: What are some of the sacrifices you've had to make to give so much to basketball?

Lindsay: There's been a lot, for me and for others. What comes to mind is missing family reunions, weddings, the birthdays of my brothers and sisters, special events like that. And for years now, being in Europe from fall to spring, I've missed Thanksgiving and Easter, although I've always gotten to come home for Christmas. To play basketball and do what I've done has been wonderful, but sacrifices come with it for sure.

Question: How has your success affected your parents and siblings?

Lindsay: They've definitely made sacrifices, too, but I think they feel it's been worth it. It's given everyone an opportunity to see parts of the world they may never have gotten to see, plus, I think just coming to the games has been fun for them. It's great after a game seeing them all excited. Having your family interested in something you're passionate about is so important. I definitely wouldn't be here today doing what I'm doing if it wasn't for my family's support.

Question: Are you comfortable being labeled a "phenom"?

Lindsay: You really can't worry about what other people think. I try not to think about it too much because I'm just a normal person who plays basketball. I relish the fact that young people look up to me and I can be a role model, but other than that, I'd rather just play basketball and have fun and not be too concerned about stuff like that. There are times when it could add pressure, too, although that just means you're playing good enough to have an expectation placed on you, which is good.

Question: Is it difficult to be on the road so much during the season?

Lindsay: You picked a good day to ask me that because I've been in Texas, Chicago, and on the East Coast in just the past week, and up at 4:30 a.m. two days in a row traveling for back-to-back games. So, yeah, it is, especially at the end of a season. The first couple road trips with a new team are more fun. There's team bonding, whether it's going out to eat before or after a game, and it's the time when you get to know all your teammates. But at the end of the season it's tougher, that's just the way it is. You've been playing for three or four months in a row and you get to the point you've had fourteen or fifteen trips, that's a lot to be on the road. Sometimes it's like seven days in a row. It's still fun to be with your teammates, and with Internet and cell phones you can still keep in touch with home, but it can get tiring, especially with back-to-back games.

Question: Are there times you don't feel like practicing? Playing in the game?

Lindsay: No, not unless I'm sore, really sore, I always like it. I especially enjoy practice, but then games are fun too because you're going for the win. Games are only like forty minutes and there are usually just a few a week, so naturally you're excited for them. There's always that excitement and passion for the game. Of course there are some days when you either don't feel well or it's been a long season, you're not quite as excited every single day to practice, but for the most part I'm always up for both practices and games.

Question: What kind of exercise routine do you maintain, on and off season?

Lindsay: To be honest, I've been in season straight for so many years I pretty much just have a practice schedule. I haven't had an off-season for five years. If I did have a couple months off, I'd shoot a lot, lift weights, do cardio on the elliptical or treadmill. I'd get a program from our strength coach on conditioning and follow that. I'd probably work out four to five times a week and take the weekends off. But since I don't have that kind of time off, practice in season gives me the amount I need to stay healthy, in shape, and maintain.

Question: Do you stick to a diet or eating regiment to feel peak?

Lindsay: Sort of, especially lately. As I've gotten older I've been focusing on nutrition and eating better to stay in shape because I want plenty more years to play. I've paid attention for a while now on what's good to eat, what's bad to eat. If you can stay lean and firm, it's going to help your career last longer and help decrease injuries. I've learned a lot more as I've gotten older because like, I'm 28, and some of the point guards coming in are 21, and even though I've got the experience, they've got young legs, so I've got to stay in shape to be able to keep up with them. I think that's something a lot of players really take to heart. But I eat pretty normal. I try to eat lots of veggies and fruits and stay away from fast food.

Question: Are there many concessions or compromises you and Ben make to keep up with both of your schedules?

Lindsay: Sure, with him playing in tournaments and me playing on the road, there are times when we go days without seeing each other. It's a big part of our lives but we work around it the best we can. We've both had to give up a lot when it comes to being home with each other and our families. It actually helps that we both are in sports because we know what it's like for the other, and are understanding, so it works. Plus, we're very grateful to have these careers.

Question: Do you feel you may have missed "normal" things growing up because of basketball?

Lindsay: It wasn't until college that I got really into basketball, so I got to do normal things growing up before that. It was just in college, then the pros, that things got a little away from normal with all the travel and being on the road, but it's a job and that happens.

Question: Would you do it all again the very same way?

Lindsay: Yeah, I would! Definitely.

Question: What would you like to add in conclusion?

Lindsay: I'd like to say that I feel very fortunate and grateful for all of my experiences, and I hope that those experiences, or things that I've said, are useful to someone else who's looking at a career in sports, or looking at a goal. I'm glad if any part of my career has set a good example. And I'd like to say thank you to all my fans reading this. You've made my career possible. I hope it's been enjoyable for you! Thank you.

Appendix: Award and Honors

"In the arena of human life the honors and rewards fall to those who show their good qualities in action."

— Aristotle

High School
A four-time honorable mention all-state selection
Led her team to three consecutive conference championships
A four-time All-Missota Conference pick
Hutchinson's all-time scoring leader with 1,996 points
Still holds many of the schools basketball records
The only Hutchinson athlete to have her number retired

College
2001
Named to the Big Ten All-Rookie Team
Team MVP
All-Big Ten honorable mention
Coaches Award

Kadidja Andersson, Leslie Hill and Lindsay with NCAA Trophy.

2002

U.S. Basketball Writers Association All-American

Team MVP

Big Ten MVP

Chicago Tribune Big Ten Player of the Year

Only player in Big-Ten history to receive five Player of the
Week awards in one season

Academic All-Big Ten

Fastest female Gopher to reach 1,000 career points, doing
so in 51 games

Verizon Academic All-District V second team

NCAA All-Midwest Regional Team

All-America Kodak/WBCA All-America honorable mention

Associated Press All-American third team honoree

Voted Favorite Female Athlete in *City Pages* Best of The Twin Cities reader's poll

Fast Break Club Award

Big Ten Player of the Year, one of only three sophomores in conference history to earn it

Won gold medal as member of the 2002 USA World Championship for Young Women Qualifying team

2002–2003

Named to the All-Big Ten first team

Selected for the Big Ten Conference All-Academic Team with a 3.42 GPA

2003

U.S. Basketball Writers Association All-American

Wade Trophy finalist

Two time winner of the Big Ten Player of the Week Award

Naismith Award finalist

Team MVP

Verizon Academic All-America third team

AP All-America second team

Academic All-District

Academic All-Big Ten

NCAA All-Midwest Regional Team

A member of U.S. gold medal-winning team at the FIBA

Gopher senior night, February 26, 2004.

World Championship for Young Women.

Kodak/WBCA All-America first team

First athlete in U of M history to have her own bobblehead

2003–2004

First Big Ten player to record back-to-back 30-point games

2004

First woman named Minneapolis *Star Tribune*'s
Sportsperson of the Year

St. Paul *Pioneer Press* Sportsperson of the Year

Wade Trophy finalist

Naismith Award finalist

Two time winner of the Big Ten Player of the Week Award

Team MVP

Kodak/WBCA All-America

Big Ten All-Academic team

Winner of the Inspiration award at the U of M's 15th Annual Scholar-Athlete Awards Banquet

NCAA All-Midwest Regional Team

Inducted into the KDUZ Hall of Fame

Fast Break Club Award

Fifth highest scorer all-time in the Big Ten Conference

Academic All-Big Ten

A unanimous all-Big Ten selection

U of M's all-time career scoring leader, male or female, with 2,285 points

Holds Minnesota career records in scoring average, games in double figures, free throws made and free throw percentage.

First player from the U of M to earn All-American honors in three different seasons (2002–2004)

The only four-time team MVP in U of M history

First Gopher women's basketball player to earn academic all-American acclaim

Most decorated player in Golden Gopher history

Her #13 jersey was retired during U of M's "Lindsay Whalen Day," January 3, and now hangs with a banner from the rafters of Williams Arena

PROFESSIONAL CAREER

2004

The first Gopher drafted by the WNBA and the highest pick (fourth) in Big Ten history at that time

Lindsay in the Aquatennial parade, 2009

U.S. Basketball Writers Association All-American

Selected to play in the historic WNBA vs. USA Basketball game at Radio City Music Hall; fan vote elected her to the starting lineup

Euroleague All-Star team

Named to the 2007–08 USA Women's Basketball National Team

2008

Selected to the First Team All-WNBA

MVP runner-up

WNBA Eastern Conference Player of the Week (May 27)

Peak Performance Award for leading the league with 5.4 assists average per game

WNBA Eastern Conference Player of the Week (July 14)

Euroleague All-Star team

Named to 2009–10 USA Basketball Women's National Team

ESPY nominee for Best WNBA Player

One of six distinguished University of Minnesota alumni grand marshals for the 2009 Homecoming parade

Euroleague All-Star team

Grand Marshall of the annual Aquatennial Torch Light Parade in Minneapolis

A few rebounds shy of becoming only the third player in WNBA history with 2500 points, 1000 rebounds, and 1000 assists

ACKNOWLEDGMENTS

Lindsay Whalen is great at what she does in large part because of who she is. It is with tremendous appreciation we acknowledge the following people who have contributed to her life, and to this book:

Neil and Kathy Whalen, a true picture of your daughter could not have been accomplished without you, your family, or Ben and his family, the Greves. A special nod goes to Lindsay's sister Katie who helped during an extra busy time in her own life, and her grandparents, Cornelius and Kathleen Whalen and Casey and Mary Ann Vilandre, all of whom were a pleasure to work with and had wonderful perspectives to offer. Aunt Mary Whalen is included in that, as are friends Emily Inglis, Kim Danlo, and neighbor Ron McGraw. They superbly represented themselves and so many others.

The professionals in her life were also all anxious to lend their thoughts and accounts of her. Many thanks to Glen Taylor and Roger Griffith of the Minnesota Lynx, Chris Sienko and Bill Tavares of the Connecticut Sun, and coaches Andy Rostberg, Pam Borton, Mike Thibault, and Cheryl Reeve. Your input has been invaluable. Bill, your extra help with facts was perfect and timely. And Pam, an additional thanks to you too and the staff at the U of M, including Dave Lindquist, Becky Bohm, Gary Bowman, and Sara Berhow, for the great pictures of Lindsay's years as a Golden Gopher. Aaron Seehusen, Public Relations Coordinator for the Lynx, thank you for doing the same work with pictures, as well as your full assistance.

Credit for more pictures and valuable glimpses of Lindsay goes to Sue Corbin, Cathy Mahowald, Karen Lueck, and Gary Cohen, all of the Fast Break Club. What a joy it was to share in your enthusiasm for Lindsay the Golden Gopher. Picture credit also goes to Kim Danlo, Lindsay herself, and, as happens, much of it fell to mom Kathy Whalen. Thank you! And thanks go to Matt McMillan, publisher of the Hutchinson *Leader*, and sports editor Eric Kraushar for their help in making sure a rounded picture of Lindsay was available for the book, and to Sophia Hantzes, the talented free lance photographer who supplied the cover photo.

Joel Maturi, a huge thank you for honoring us with the foreword. It's never an easy job to put into words the accomplishment of another, but you did it beautifully. Also paying homage to Lindsay's abilities and personality were the gracious media: John Mons, Joel Niemeyer, Joe Schmit, Eric Nelson, Larry Fitzgerald, Sr., and Mike Max. Many thanks to all of you.

This book would not have come into being if it wasn't for Norton Stillman and John Toren of Nodin Press. Their enthusiasm for it and the expertise they wield is incredible, and has produced a wonderful book. Helping in that process too has been to William Bundy of Riverview Media Partners, offering his ongoing assistance and marketing skills, and Boris Lelchitski, President of Sports International Group, Inc. and Lindsay's agent.

And lastly, a special and heartfelt thanks to you, Lindsay. Thank you for your generous time and help in making this a valuable account of you, and for all you have given us in your game play and in your great example of what it means to be a person of character. It has been a privilege to know you and to write this book as a tribute.

R. S. Oatman is an author and artist, currently living in Wisconsin. Her first book, *UniverSoul Ways,* has movie rights optioned, and her upcoming series, *The Highland Six,* chronicles the fictional lives of six former college roommates as they individually and together navigate the changing times for women from the seventies to today.

Her painting, *Unity & Spirit,* a depiction of a rescue scene from the 1989 Loma Prieta earthquake in San Francisco, has been used and reproduced into commemorative items for anniversary ceremonies of the devastating quake, and hangs in the Office of Emergency Services in Oakland, CA.

She is the proud mother of Shawn and Julie, and loving grandmother to Molly, Hannah, Max, and Mason.